Performance Appraisal is Dead – Long Live Performance Contracting

Roelf Woldring

"Shape the Future, Don't Appraise the Past." ™

Copyright
Workplace Competence International Limited
WCI Press

114 Church Street East
P.O. Box 2906
Elora, Ontario, Canada
N0B 1S0
1-519-846-0100

March 2013

Parts of this book have appeared in the past,
in this or modified forms, on the following web sites.

www.wecrut3.com
www.wciltd.com

Note:

If you are viewing this book online as a PDF, you will be able to click on the underlined words to go to the relevant web page. If you are reading it in print, you may have to entered the associated url into your browser or use a search engine to find out more about the underlined reference.

Introduction

Hr. Hobie Has His Way

"Roelf – sit down and sign this at the bottom". With these words, Mr. Hobie, the office clerk, introduced me to performance appraisals. It was my first job. I was16. For three months, I had been delivering mail, making Gestetner offset and Xerox photocopies, and running out for lunches for the lawyers in the large law firm where I was the office boy. When I had been hired, no one had told me that I was on probation. But now here I was looking at a form with my name on it and the title "End of Probation Performance Appraisal" across the top.

Being around lawyers and their secretaries has taught me a few things. By then, I knew that you don't sign it till you have read it.

"Can I take a minute or so to read this please?" I asked Mr. Hobie. He frowned and say angrily "You don't need too. Just sign it. I rated you o.k. Sign it here now." He pointed to a line on the bottom of the page.

With a sinking feeling in the pit of my stomach, I did. He took the form off to the office manager. By two weeks later, I had found a junior clerk job at a much larger organization. It was not until the day that I started the job, that I realized how insulted I had been by Mr. Hobie's behavior.

My experience with Mr. Hobie's approach to performance appraisal was a taste of things to come. Since then, I have been performance appraised many times. It always felt arbitrary. I was never told what I would be appraised on. Performance appraisal was something that was "done" to me by the person for whom I worked. It was an annual rite that really reminded me of who was who in the power scheme of things. I became really clear about that the first time a peer of mine lost her job as a result of a negative appraisal.

I talked to the my colleagues at work and my friends how they experienced the performance appraisal process. The perceptions among us at the working level were clear.

"Don't upset the boss, or else he will get you at PA time."

All the bosses were men in the first years of my career. Everyone felt that the performance appraisal process was arbitrary and unfair. But it was what it was, and if you wanted to keep your job, you just accepted it. If you did not like how your boss treated you at PA time, then you knew that you had to find another job."

Then I became a boss. Suddenly, I had to do performance appraisals on the folks who worked for me. I have gone back to graduate school by then. Safe in the halls of academia, I read a few books on the design, purpose and function of performance appraisal systems. Performance appraisal was supposed to be about managing performance and helping staff develop. It was not supposed to be about power. Based on my reading, I was determined that the PA experience for my direct reports was going to be different.

I invited my direct reports to talk to me during PA sessions. I wanted discussion about what they were doing and how they could improve. I wanted to get them involved in planning their own skill development.

Somehow, my intentions never translated into reality. The whole atmosphere of the annual performance appraisal meeting was poisoned by the rating that came at the end. Since bonus amounts were tied to these ratings, not one of my direct reports had a lot of patience for what I was trying to do. Sure, some of my folks "humored" me. After all, I was the boss. But mostly we were relieved if the whole PA thing got done quickly and was out of the way for another year.

I am a pretty determined type of guy. I was not going to give up. I hit upon the idea of having the folks who worked for me do their own PA. They would self appraise themselves. I would do mine of them independently. We would both fill out the forms and make a rating. We would exchange our filled out forms and meet. I thought that this would be a solid basis for us and talk and reconcile any differences. I was a naïve, optimistic fool.

The first time I did this was with a fellow who was clearly one of the best performers that I have ever had working for me. He took to this task diligently, like he did everything. I put a lot of thought into writing clean crisp comments on the results he had delivered in the past year. I tried to point out useful opportunities for improvement. I laid out a development plan that I thought for help him grow and become capable of taking on my job. Finally, I rated him 5 out of 5.

Then I read his self appraisal. It was terse to say the least. It understated everything he had done during the year as factually as he could. He gave no thought to how he might improve. He completely ignored the development plan section. Finally, he rated himself 3 – average – out of 5.

We met – for about three hours. I learned more about the demoralizing impact of an annual performance appraisal that I ever wanted to know. His final comment at the end our meeting really floored me.

> "That was that the most humiliating experience I have had in a
> long time. Your are the boss. You have the power to rate me
> however you want, regardless of what I think of my performance.
> Asking me to appraise myself feels like a set up game to me. It is

bad enough get appraised and rated by you. Having to do it to myself really pointed out how powerless I feel in the boss – subordinate thing. Please don't ask me to do it again."

He clearly thought he was performing at better than an average level. But he had not wanted to take the risk that I did not agree with him. He was concerned about the possibility that I would rate him less than he had rated himself. He felt that this could poison the working relationship we had experienced during the last year. So he deliberately rated himself lower than he thought he deserved. But he could also not bring himself to rate himself lower than average. We talked it all through. I thought that I had overcome his concerns and reservations. Three months later, he was gone, having found another job.

The meetings with my other direct reports did not last as long. They were either sullen or afraid. They did not talk much. Or they were unrealistic about their own performance, seriously over rating their performance. When that happened, we were immediately thrown into open conflict.

I never repeated this experience. For a year or two after this, I just colluded with the existing PA process, filling out the forms, walking through the meetings, accepting the fact that it was part of a manager's job. I really disliked doing it.

Then I rebelled. As usual, my conviction that there had to be a better way came to my aid. I started to look forward, not backwards when thinking about performance with respect to my direct reports. I started to talk to my folks about what I hoped they would achieve. I start to write my expectations down, asking myself "How will I know that this person has achieved this objective? What will I be seeing? What will other people be saying?"

I shared the results with them. Sometimes they just accepted this. But often they pointed out ways in which my expectations could be made clearer, or added metrics that made more sense. I had started the process that led to this book.

When I started to performance contract, rather than performance appraise, my organizations thrived. The folks who worked for me blew me away again and again. They consistently performed. Often they exceeded my expectations, and even their own.

Well, mostly … there were a few folks that did not respond this way. They resented the "performance pressure", as they put it, that performance contracting put on them. Sometimes these folks self selected themselves out of the process, i.e. they found other jobs. Or they underperformed, and they knew it because the metrics we were both using to track their performance results were perfectly clear. We usually came to a "departure" arrangement that was mutual, and much less expensive than a traditional "firing".

I am not the only manager who has had this experience. If you read "First, Break All the Rules: What the World's Great Managers Do Differently"[1], you will find that they all set and communicate clear expectations for the people who work for them. Performance contracting is all about setting clear, mutually agreed to expectations. But it also adds one thing more. As well as negotiating / setting performance expectations, performance contracting clarifies the metrics – the "how we will measure" the achievement of those expectations. Performance contracting allows people to self evaluate against clear expectations and do one of the following:

- initiate corrective actions – which is a self rewarding activity,

- or ask for help – which provides the necessary motivation for effective coaching and professional development,

- or they face the reality that they are not delivering, which allows the manager to raise the issue in a coaching conversation, the first step in dealing effectively with low performance situations.

In the work world in which I developed my career, the era of baby boomers, there were lots of people in the work force. The entry of women swelled the numbers even more. Managers could play power games like the ones inherent in performance appraisal and survive as managers.

Those days are gone. Global competition and the demographic shrinking of the work force are relentless pressures. The bar has been raised. What was the exceptional in the past is now the needed norm. You must inspire your staff by communicating clear expectations and giving them the capability to measure their own result delivery. If you do not, one of two things will happen,.

First, if you share your inability to do this with most of the other managers in your organization, your organization will disappear.

Or second, if you are one of the few managers in your organization who do not do this, you will disappear, at least from your organization.

What is this book about?

This book contain 3 sections. They can be read independently, or as a whole. Each section is described briefly below.

---

[1] ISBN 978-0-684-85286-7   The cover of this 1999 book reads "Based on in-depth interviews by the Gallup Organization of over 80,000 managers in over 400 companies – the largest study of its kind ever undertaken". The authors, Marcus Buckingham and Curt Coffman, have done an excellent job of taking the research result and putting them into language any manager can first, understand, and then second, put into action on the job. See http://businessjournal.gallup.com/content/1144/first-break-all-rules-book-center.aspx for an excellent introduction to the book.

Section Title	What it contains	How it came about
"Shape the Future" Performance Contracting"	A set of 8 articles explaining performance contracting, why it beats performance appraisal hands down as a means of engaging and motivating staff.	Written as blog entries on performance management via performance contracting.
"Avoiding Bad Hires: The Steep Cost of Hiring Mistakes"	Performance based recruiting, how it works What kind of hiring mistakes can you make How to avoid bad hires	Original published as a blog entry, the pieces has expanded over time to take into account performance based recruiting techniques.
"Delivering Results: Performance Contracting and Personal Development in Your Organization"	A workbook written for the leaders and professional staff in an organization that moved from performance appraisal to performance contracting plus periodic personal performance evaluation as a means to determine bonuses. A personal development component was added to help managers and direct reports plan skill development activities.	The original version as created as part of a client assignment. The engagement agreement allowed me to make the generic version of this work book made available to other organizations and individuals.

I have managed people for over 30 years. In many ways, what I have written here is the result of what I have learned from the many talented, inspiring people who helped me understand what it is to lead. Thank You.

Section One

Shape The Future:
Performance Contracting

**Move your organization
from the drag of
performance appraisal
to the joy of
performance contracting**

Introduction to Shape the Future: Performance Contracting

The articles in this short book, along with the Internet based voice over presentations and other Internet based resources that are referred to in these pages, can help you become a performance contracting wizard.

**Engage your staff,
no matter which generation they belong to:**

**Baby Boomer,
Generation X,
Generation Y,
Or generations yet to come.**

Start performance contracting today. These pages will show you how.

These articles are independent of one another. Some of them are "how to" guides. Others show the benefits of moving to performance contracting, based on work place psychology or experience in the work place.

Pick and choose the order in which you use them. Treat them as a "surf-able" personal development resource that will help you be a more effective manager of others, increasing their engagement in their work and their productivity.

You can also read this articles as a guide to why your organization needs to move from a performance appraising culture to a performance contracting one.

Versions of some of these articles first appeared in my blog "Reflections on Business, People and Life" (http://roelfwoldring.wordpress.com).

1. Why you need to be a performance contracting manager?

Performance Contracting is the key to Employee Engagement and Organizational Excellence.

The HR and business press is full of articles about how Generation X, Generation Y and the next Generation now entering the work force are different from the Baby Boomers who are about to retire. But in one way they are not so different. Employee satisfaction surveys still tell us, like they have for the past twenty years, that employees do not believe that performance appraisal helps them improve their performance.

So why are we as managers not listening? There are a variety of reasons. Some have to do with organizational inertia. Some have to do with the fact that managers appreciate the re-enforcement of their power over direct reports inherent in performance appraisal. But most importantly, we, as managers, really haven't had the business support systems that we need to move from appraising past performance to contracting for future performance delivery.

Contracting for performance with our direct reports requires that we commit to the regular independent delivery of feedback to them. That feedback has to be based on agreed upon performance metrics relevant to each of our direct reports. In the majority of cases, these metrics will come from automated business applications that we now use to run our business. The cost effective delivery of such information is now possible with the current information technology.

The business tools that we need are finally there. Now all we need to do is change our attitudes. We need to stop appraising people. We need to stop telling them what they did and did not do in the past. We need to stop rating them on an evaluation scale that invariably involves subjective judgment.

Long Live Performance Contracting

We need to move to contracting about their future performance with them. We need to help them get crystal clear on what it is they are expected to deliver. We tell them exactly how we will evaluate whether or not they deliver the results they contract to deliver. Finally, we need to make sure that they have access to the data on these metrics independently of us, directly from the automated business applications that we both use to do our work.

For the organizations that do this, magic happens. Most people want to do well. Most people want to contribute to the organization for which they work. Most people, when they get regular independent feedback on how they're doing, will take steps to correct their performance when they go off track. The best of them will strive to exceed their contracted delivery levels.

That's the essence of performance contracting for excellence. It is also the basis of effective boss – direct report coaching. Together, these two are the key to improving people engagement in the workplace. That engagement is now, and will be ever more crucial, in the current and coming competition for skills and talent.

Let us as managers demonstrate to the people who work for us that we can do what we expect them to do: **listen to feedback**. Let us take what we've been hearing on employee satisfaction survey after employee satisfaction survey seriously. Let's start shaping the future, and stop appraising the past. Commit yourself to performance contracting with your direct reports today.

_____

The following link will take you to an Internet Browser voice over presentation that expands on this article.

<u>Why Performance Contracting?</u>

Either click on the link, or copy and paste the following URL into your Internet Brower.

<u>http://www.wciltd.com/pdfquark/PCWhy/clevelpcwhyv2c/player.html</u>)

2. Engage your staff: 7 steps to becoming a performance contracting wizard

Are you, like thousands of managers, dreading the performance appraisals that you need to do at the end of every year? Just about every survey of working professionals that asks questions about performance appraisal document the discontent that people feel with the performance appraisal process.

So how do you make this better? How do you avoid the year end performance appraisal blues? Simple, really. Make a resolution to move from performance appraisal to performance contracting. Here's how to do it in seven steps.

Start by making a list of the people for work for you. For each one, brainstorm the things that they do for you. Use the outline facility in Word or an outliner software tool or paper and pencil, whatever works for you.

Once you have this initial list, re-organize it until you have between 3 and 7 main responsibilities for each person. It's hard to work with more. If your list for an individual is longer, group things together until you have the 3 to 7 you need. Note the similarities between people. That will help you in the next step.

Take an individual on your list. Imagine that this person is going to do a great job on each of these 3 to 7 responsibilities in the coming year. Visualize this. Run an internal film or set of pictures if that works for you. Ask yourself the following questions about each of the 3 to 7 responsibilities.

"Jack (or whatever the person's name is) is doing a great job at xxxx (fill in one of the responsibilities in your list). So what will I be:

Seeing – what's showing me that … (the person's name) … is doing a great at this?

Hearing – who's telling me that that …. (the person's name) … is doing a great job at this? What are they telling me?"

Translate what you are imagining - seeing and hearing - into a single statement – a measure or metric that lets you and others know that this person is doing a great job on this responsibility. Ask yourself the following question as you do this.

"Will I be hearing and seeing this every day, every week, every quarter, ...?"

That adds an important time dimension. The shorter, the better. Keep time dimensions under a quarter; monthly or weekly metrics are far more useful.

Today, many of these metrics are available from the automated business applications that we use to do work. Make sure that the person has acces to this information, so that they will be getting constant feedback on how she or he is doing directly from these computer applications.

Organize your results into a single page for each person. List the 5 to 7 responsibilities. Put the appropriate measure or metric below each one. Title the page "Draft performance contract for … the person's name." Make two copies.

Arrange a meeting with each person. Plan for about an hour Give each person a copy of the draft performance contract before the meeting, so that they have time to read it. Meet with each person separately. Work through the draft performance contract together. Make sure the individual is clear about each item and each measure. Listen to any issues the individual has about any item. If these concerns help clarify this person's performance objectives and make the measures even more concrete and specific, modify the page to take this into account.

When you have done this with each person, you have negotiated a forward looking performance contract for each person.

Turn each modified draft into a final version. Make two copies of it. Sign both. Get each individual to sign both copies of their personal performance contract. Take one for yourself. Give the person the other copy.

Don't underestimate the power of the ritual involved in signing these personal performance contracts. Ritual is an important way in which human beings signal commitment. Make sure that the signing process has the appropriate weight and ceremony.

There is an 8th step. It follows easily from the previous 7, and is really of a consequence of them than a step in its own right. Do this, and you are on your way to a hassle free performance review at year end.

Schedule a meeting once a month with each person who works for you. Bring your copies of that person's personal performance contract. As you review it together, ask yourselves:

"Am I seeing and hearing what we thought I would be seeing and hearing on each metric? Are the measures being met?"

"If yes, great -.let's keep going".
"If no, what can we do to get back on track?"

There, you have stopped performance appraising and become a performance contractor. Instead of looking back and evaluating, you are looking ahead and coaching.

You will find that your folks appreciate knowing what they have to and how it will be measured. They will probably surprise you by exceeding some of their measures. They will be engaged in their jobs. They will be evaluating their own performance, and seeking to improve it.

Occasionally, this will not happen. You may have a person who consistently does not achieve his or her contracted performance metrics. You now have a factual basis to engage that person in problem solving dialogue about this. When this happens, you are acting as an effective, focused coach. If the individual does not respond positively, you also have a factual basis for moving to job re-assignment, job simplification or even termination.

3. Ho, Ho, Ho – It's the Season for Performance Appraisals

I asked Susan, my horse sharing friend, what was going on with her as we drove over the stable to work Hamish (He is a Canadian gelded horse who weight about 1500 pounds, and is very smart as horses go.)

She groaned, and said,

> "It is performance appraisal time. I just don't like doing them.
> They always kind of spoil the year end at work for me."

Susan is not aware that I write and consult on performance contracting. Her comments reflected unhappiness with the performance appraisal process that I have heard from countless managers and direct reports.

"Just what are you doing?", I asked, knowing that there was a good chance I would hear things that reflected the reality experienced by millions of subordinates and mangers. She replied.

> "Well, I'm working on my own appraisal. At the same, I doing the
> ones I need to do for the folks who work for me. It always feels
> like a game to me. I haven't had a single conversation this year
> with my boss about what I'm supposed to do and how she is
> going to measure my performance. And now she asks me to

write up my own performance appraisal and rate myself. I know it's tied to her concerns about how year end bonuses will be allocated. She's done this to me every year that I have worked for her. It's all a big set up game."

Susan was obviously discouraged. You could tell from her voice tone that she really didn't enjoy talking about this. I decided to leave it alone when she continued on.

"They tell us that the performance appraisal at our company is objective and based on performance dialogue that we should be having all year. I try to do that with my subordinates. Because I hate not being clear on how I'm going to be measured myself, I try to be as clear about this with them as I can. Also, I know that they know that their annual bonuses are tied to their performance appraisal ratings. That makes all of us anxious. Money is money - we all can use more, especially at Christmas."

Seeing that she was willing to go on, I asked, "Do your subordinates feel differently about performance appraisal based on what you do?" She responded,

"It's the power tripping and game playing that really gets to me. We all know it's about money. The performance appraisal rating we each get directly determines the size of our annual bonus."

She looked out the car window and went on.

"I get along reasonably well with my boss during the year, but it always seems to fall apart at year end. She asks me to complete my performance appraisal form and rate myself. I already know that she's already decided what rating she is going to give me. I also know it has more to do with how she wants to spread out the bonus money she has over the folks she has working for her. She clearly enjoys the power position that this puts her in."

She sighed, looked at me and continued.

"My final rating is going to be based on a bunch of things, none of which have anything to do with my real performance. She will rate me based on who she wants to reward and how she feels about me compared to everyone else. So this puts me in a real bind. I struggle with it for days before I finally stop thinking about what I did during the year and just try to guess at what I think she wants me to rate me."

Making sure my non-verbal cues were sympathetic, I asked "what about the performance appraisals you have to do for the people who work for you?"

"That's just it", she responded, sighing again and looking out the car window, before she turned back to me.

> "I know my boss's real concern is about how she's going to distribute the pool of bonus dollars that have been allocated to her. Part of that relates to who gets what among my subordinates. She's not going to engage in real dialogue with me about what they did during the year. Sure, she will go through the motions, but she finalizes my ratings of them based on how she wants to spread out the money. I sense that she's doing calculations in her head about this the whole time we are reviewing my ratings of my direct reports. And she always does this before she tells me what my own rating is going to be. If I disagree with her about the rating for one of my folks, I know she will pull down my own rating. So I don't. That makes me feel like a traitor, especially to the folks who have really performed this year, if she decides to rate them less than they deserve."

"What does that do to your relationships with the folks who work for you?" I asked. Susan replied with real bitterness in her voice.

> "Poisons them, quite frankly, at least until everybody knows what bonuses they are going to get. They know perfectly well how my boss handles this. It is an open secret no one talks about. They often play up to her more than they pay attention to me. The final ratings that my people get have more to do with how effectively they manage my boss's feelings about them than the work they do for me."

"Sound frustrating", I replied in an encourage tone of voice. Susan's voice tone became hard as she responded. I could sense that she was being careful in her choice of words.

> "I suspect the fact that some of my folks, who are good-looking members of the opposite gender, really know how to subtly, without being obvious or foolish, influence her feelings about them. Again, it is almost an open family secret. Everyone knows it. Nobody ever talks about it. But everyone knows. And it is all o.k., because nobody ever takes it over the line whether it is obvious abusive or inappropriate. I hate performance appraisal time."

Susan was clearly unhappy about all of this. Since I didn't want spoil our working time together with Hamish, so I changed the topic to how we will work with him today. Susan responded with relief.

Susan's feelings about performance appraisal are not unusual. Survey after survey, done both by outside HR experts and by internal HR departments, have shown that most managers and staff dislike and do not trust their company's performance appraisal process. They deal with it, particularly in light of the fact that so many companies tie annual or other bonuses to performance appraisal ratings. But very few survey respondents believe that performance appraisal has much to do with people's actual performance on the jobs. They also make it clear that they find performance appraisal a de-motivating process.

There are several things that companies can do to avoid this annual feeling of malaise.

If your organization insists on using a performance appraisal process, try to schedule them so they are not tied to the calendar year end. Scheduling performance appraisals on the anniversary of employment dates for instance avoids this concentration of unhappiness at year end.

Make sure that you use a performance contracting process that aligns with your organization's performance appraisal process. Since performance contracting looks ahead, you will clarify what your expect your direct reports to do during the year. You will have concrete results on specific measures to defend your year end performance appraisal rating of your subordinates. That will decrease the viability of the kind of "game playing" that Susan experienced with her boss.

Your organization can also do some things that reduce the negative impact of year end performance appraisal on morale and motivation. A crucial one relates to the way in which the organization designs its bonus compensation scheme. Organizations wanting to avoid the year end performance /appraisal frenzy and blues structure their bonus scheme so that it has two or more components.

One organization has the following bonus compensation scheme. Although each portion of the bonus is smaller than the one time annual bonus paid by their competitors, their employee satisfaction surveys indicate that their employees are much happier with this structure.

A company performance bonus paid out to everyone in early February. The amount is related to their annual salary. It is based on the total company's performance on corporate financial and operational measures in the past calendar (= fiscal) year. These targets are communicated to everyone as part of the annual planning process early in the relevant year.

A team bonus which is paid out all of the members of each team in December, based on each team's achievement of a set of predetermined team targets. Every member of the team receives a portion of this bonus amount based on the ratio of their annual salary to the total annual salary for the team. These performance targets are

also developed and communicated as part of the annual planning process early in the year.

An individual bonus directly related to the person's performance appraisal ranking is paid out (or not) based on the person's personal performance appraisal rating. Performance appraisals are scheduled based on the anniversary of each individual's original employment date. This bonus amount is paid in the month following appraisal completion.

As we arrived at the stable, Susan sighed and said,

> "You know, I would just like to know what I am supposed to do, and how I am going to be measured on it. It would get rid of the games."

Susan and millions of others agree. Yet somehow, organizations are stuck in a performance appraisal rut. As a result, "Ho, Ho, Ho" means anything but employee satisfaction and engagement during each year end's performance appraisal season.

4. Why you need an independent honest broker to facilitate C-Level performance contracting?

As a CEO or Board member, you depend on the advice of lawyers when you enter into complex contracts with your external business partners. You need equivalent independent advice when you enter into personal performance contracts with your C-Level executives. They are the individuals whose talent and execution leads to your business success.

Depending on intuition and personal feelings does not lead to clear executive level performance contracts. We evolved as tribal beings, not as organization participants. Our approach to leadership is based on our evolved tribal instincts and capabilities, not on a rational approach to defining leadership expectations.

We have learned to move beyond our instinctive approach when we shape legal contracts between organizations. We can do the same when it comes to formulating performance contracts with corporate leaders.

Often the thing that gets in the way of developing C-level performance contracts is a lack of time. C-level executives are extremely busy people. Time is their single most scare resource.

An external "honest broker" facilitator who takes on the task of developing C-Level performance contracts eases much of this dilemma. The cost involved is minimal compared to the benefits for the organization. The C-level leaders involved are energized and focused by the resulting performance clarity. They are free to put all of their energy into delivering the organization's desired results.

Long Live Performance Contracting

The executive's actual performance contract is the basis for a comprehensive, clear "cascade down" in the executive's reporting group. C-level executives guide, direct and delegate more than they personally do. Sharing relevant portions of an executive's personal performance contract with appropriate direct reports clarifies their own persona performance expectations in a powerful way. They are the individuals who engage with staff to achieve these performance goals.

An experienced executive performance contracting facilitator guides the development and the negotiation of C-Level performance contracts in ways that are beneficial to the executive and the executive's "boss". Acting as the honest broker, the facilitator ensures that both sides have a clear idea of what is expected and how it will be measured. The facilitator contributes by selecting, designing or refining performance metrics that they relate specifically to each performance objective in the executive's contract. The facilitator also takes on the writing task, saving both the executive and the executive's boss considerable time.

Being an honest broker requires more than an ability to communicate clearly and to write well. The facilitator has to have been there. She or he must have experience as a CEO and C-Level executive to "know" what it takes to be a C-Level leader.

C-level performance contracting honest is the last and most necessary step in effective strategic planning. During the personal performance contracting process, an experienced honest broker facilitator takes care to ensure that the "strat plan" is translated into aligned personal action for each of the C-Level executives.

The strategic plan may be formal – written out, or informal - the result of a dialogue that occurs among the inner circle of an organization's senior leaders. However, unless it becomes concrete in the personal performance contracts of the C-level leaders, the strategic plan cannot cascade down through the organization in a way that aligns the efforts of all the staff. Staff may understand it in very different, non-aligned ways when they think about what it means for their own jobs.

This aligning of performance expectations is the greatest value delivered by an effective C-Level performance contracting facilitator. The honest broker's only stake is the performance contracting process is producing clarity. As a result, she or he can see where there are gaps and disconnects among the C-Level executive's personal performance goals and close them.

Most organizations assume that executives are capable of translating strategic plans into personal action. They are right. Executives will. But the organization takes a risk. Each executive operates out of a "personal, often implicit" version of the strategy. Alignment among the C-Level executives may occur, but often it does not.

Forward-looking, aligned C-Level personal performance contracts create great clarity of purpose in an organization. This energizes not only the C-Level executives, but the whole organization. The result is a forward-looking performance contracting organization that values personal delivery, self evaluation, and coordinated action.

———————

The voice over Internet browser presentation below provides more detail on the how this is done.

C-Level Performance Contracting: Getting It Done (A How To Guide)

This is a voice over Browser based presentation available at: http://www.wciltd.com/pdfquark/clevelpchowto/clevelpchowto/player.html

Copy this URL and paste it into your Internet Browser if the above link does not work for you.

———————

The following page contains a template that was developed specifically to guide the development C-Level Performance Contracts for CEO's.

Not every CEO will have performance objectives in every cell. By using a framework such as this as a checklist, the honest broker facilitator will cover every aspect of a CEO's role. Systematic use of this template increases the effectiveness and the efficiency of the C-Level Performance Contract preparation process.

The template is followed by the slides from a short presentation on C-Level Performance Contracting.

———————

C-Level Performance Contracts: Task and Measures Development Grid

C-Level Performance Contracting

Tasks and Measures Development Grid

By noting which cells need deeper exploration and performance requirement clarification, we create an effective guide to the efficient development of a specific Executive Performance Contract.

Not every C-Level Executive will have performance requirements in all of these cells.

"Shape the Future, Don't Appraise the Past"™

Executive Roles	Board, including Chair	Direct Reports	"Whole Organization"	Customers	Suppliers	Bankers & Investors	Regulators	...	...
Symbol - Communicator									
FIGUREHEAD: Handles ceremonial and symbolic duties as head of the organization									
SPOKESPERSON: Communicates to the outside world on performance, possibilities and policies									
DISSEMINATOR: Transmits factual and value based information to relevant players									
Leader									
LEADER: Fosters an effective work environment. Selects, motivates and develops direct reports.									
Sponsors's actions to meet short term / long run talent needs of organization.									
RESOURCE ALLOCATOR: Controls and authorizes the use of organizational resources (physical and intellectual property assets, talent and $)									
DISTURBANCE HANDLER: Identifies, addresses and resolves / rectifies unexpected events and organizational breakdowns									
Information Manager									
MONITOR: Gathers and organizes internal and external information relevant to the organization.									
LIASION: Develops and maintains network of external contacts to gather information									
Strategist									
PLANNER: Initiates and shapes the development of business plans that achieve organizational goals in short term (1 to 2 years) and long run (>2 years)									
ENTREPRENEUR: Initiates product and process change that increases effectiveness / efficiency in the organization									
NEGOTIATOR: Strategizes, leads and participates in negotiation activities with other organizations and individuals									

Executive: _____ Title: _____ Date: _____

Performance Contracting Facilitator: _____

Copyright 2011 Workplace Competence International Limited, Elora, Ontario, Canada. V3 with acknowledgement to the work of Henry Mintzberg, *The Nature of Managerial Work*, 1973

C-Level Performance Contracts: Why Bother (presentation slides)

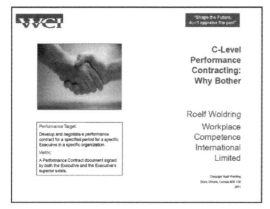

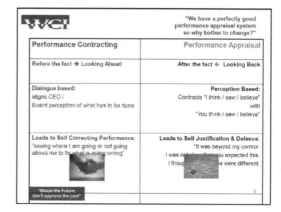

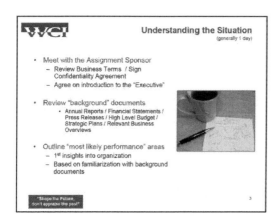

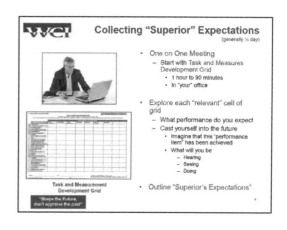

C-Level Performance Contracts: Why Bother (presentation slides - continued)

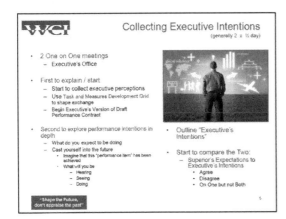

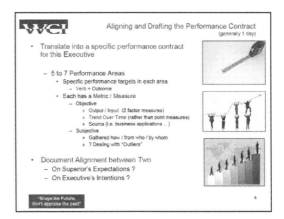

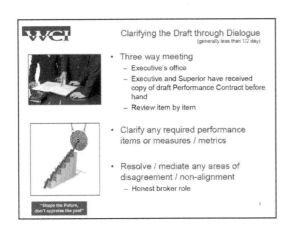

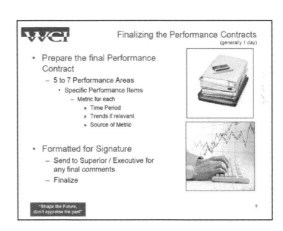

C-Level Performance Contracts: Why Bother (presentation slides - continued)

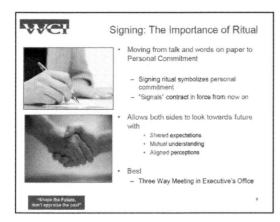

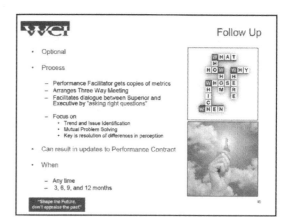

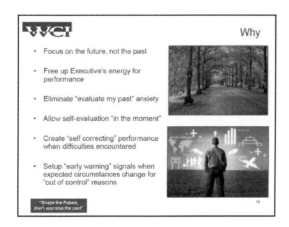

5. How to "manage progress", nature "appreciation" and engage your employees at work?

Harvey Schachter's annual column on the best business books of the year in Toronto's Globe and Mail newspaper is one of the better reads on what's what in business publishing. He has just listed his top ten business books of 2011[2].

His first pick was "The Progress Principle: Using Small Wins To Ignite Joy, Engagement and Creativity at Work"[3].

As I read it, I am reminded of the fact that employees have been telling us for decades what managers need to do to inspire excellence in them at work. The question that I always ask myself when I read books like this is "Are we as managers prepared to listen? Or do we let our power position as managers convince us that we simply know better than our employees what they need in order to excel?"

---

[2] See http://www.theglobeandmail.com/report-on-business/careers/management/management-book-excerpts/top-10-business-books-of-2011/article2270068/.

[3] See http://www.progressprinciple.com

But maybe this is the wrong question? Maybe we are listening as managers. Our problem might be that responding effectively to what we hear from employees might be "harder" than simply saying the things and behaving in the ways recommended in "The Progress Principle". It may not be as easy to "manage" progress and "nature" appreciation as books like this make out.

Achieving result in an organization requires that we all share a "systematic" way of managing performance and results delivery as well appreciating and encouraging one another. Mangers need to be able to ensure that their direct reports get performance feedback that measures progress, including negative feedback. At the same time, managers need to "encourage and appreciate" the individuals who work for them. One need cannot override or replace the other. As Jim Collins says in "Good to Great"[4], it is a matter of "AND not OR."

Performance contracting allows this "AND". Performance contracting takes into account some complex psychological realities about the way that people behave at work.

Every one has an internal mental model of their job. It guides us as we do the day-to-day things we do at work.

Our internal model of our job operates concurrently at the conscious, pre-conscious, and instinctive levels. Emotional intelligence has made us all aware that we don't just function at the conscious level at work. Our mental abilities span a complex of ability systems that include many pre-conscious and instinctive components. Some of these ability systems have evolved to process the complex interpersonal messaging that allows us to collaborate and work with others. Much of this messaging is non-verbal.

When we become part of a work group, we naturally build up a "mental model" of our jobs that guides us in the work that we do each day. Most of the time, we are not consciously aware of the fact that we are doing this. We simply do it. This model allows us to fit our personal work place activities into the "interlocked patterns of repetitive work"[5] that get things done in an organization.

Individuals build up internal models of their job through interaction with all of the people with whom they work, not just the people to whom they report.

Even the most solitary individual contributor at work does not work in a social vacuum. By definition, working in an organization means working with others at all levels to accomplish shared objectives.

---

[4] See http://www.jimcollins.com/article_topics/articles/good-to-great.html

[5] See http://www.wciltd.com/pdfquark/LearnOrgIT/learningorgworkflowv1.pdf for more on how this works in organizations.

Performance contracting brings the "what am I supposed to achieve" – the gaol components of our internal models of work - into conscious consideration.

As manager and direct report talk together during performance contract, the goal components of the direct reports internal model of work become explicit. They are shaped in the dialogue the direct report has with her or his boss.

Without such a dialogue, direct reports develop the goal components of their internal model of work in response to the behaviour patterns they engage in with our co-workers and their boss. They have a sense of "what you are supposed to achieve" that derives in part from the goal elements of their co-worker's own internal models of work.

As direct reports negotiate these goals with their boss, they are confirming or replacing these 'developed implicitly through interaction with co-workers" elements of their personal job model. The "what I am supposed to do" parts of their internal model of their role become an open shared "expectation" framework negotiated between themselves and their boss.

Once this dialogue is done, and boss and direct report sign the performance contract, direct reports start to re-shape the other elements of their internal model of work to align with their performance contract. Their now explicit negotiated performance objectives are the framework that they use to dynamically re-shape the "how to I relate to my co-worker" elements of their internal model of work. Direct reports take steps, often unconscious and instinctively shaped steps, to ensure that the "who do I need to interact with and how do I need to interact with them" elements of their guiding model of work are aligned with their negotiated objectives.

Direct reports do this dynamically, using all of their ability systems, including those that operate at the pre-conscious and instinctive levels.

Performance contracting focuses on negotiating shared performance metrics. The information needed to populate such performance metrics need to be independently available to both manager and direct report.

Much of this information will come from the automated business systems used by today's organizations to do their work. Organizations simply need to take steps to ensure that direct reports can access the information needed by the performance metrics in their personal performance contracts.

Once this is in place, the dynamics between "boss and direct report" change in a fundamental and qualitative way. The manager is now free to do all of the things recommended in "The Progress Principle".

The manager is no longer the only source of "performance evaluation information". It comes to the direct report regularly, as part of the day-to-day process of doing one's work. Direct reports measure their delivery on their objectives by seeing the trends in their performance metrics.

The direct reports self evaluate performance through out the performance period (usually a year).

When things go off track, direct reports can take corrective action.

They may reach out to their peers for help and advice. They may engage their manager in coaching dialogue.

The manager is free to "encourage progress" and "nurture through appreciation" since the manager no longer delivers "subjective" evaluations of the person's performance. These behaviours on the part of the manager are no longer experienced as "game playing" by the direct report.

If the direct report's performance difficulties continue over time, the manager can become more energetic in initiating problem solving.

Since the need to do so is defined by the trend in the direct report's performance metrics , the direct report now experiences the manager's praising, encouraging and problem solving behaviours as true coaching – as messages that motivated by a desire to "help me to do my best".

Every manager should encourage progress and nurture through appreciation. However, organizations that embrace forward-looking performance contracting create relationships dynamics between manager and direct report in which such behaviors on the part of the manager have true pay off. Performance contracting turns a "prescriptive – behave in this way" into a natural, congruent element of the productive working dynamics between manager and direct reports.

Nurture Through Appreciation
Questionnaire

Use the following checklist to see how your behavior as a manager relates to three nurturing direct reports best practices.

Meeting Delivery Targets

1 When one of your direct reports delivers a task or deliverable on or ahead of schedule, you:

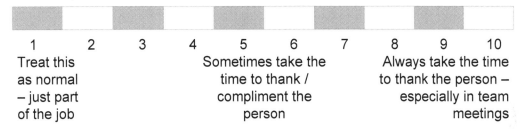

1	2	3	4	5	6	7	8	9	10
Treat this as normal – just part of the job				Sometimes take the time to thank / compliment the person			Always take the time to thank the person – especially in team meetings		

Showing Initiative

2. When one of your direct reports initiates and does a task or completes something that is not a normal part of their job, you:

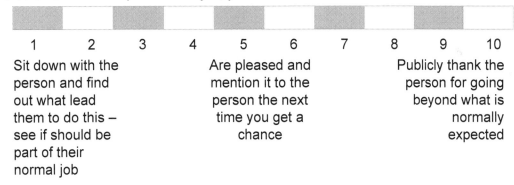

1	2	3	4	5	6	7	8	9	10
Sit down with the person and find out what lead them to do this – see if should be part of their normal job				Are pleased and mention it to the person the next time you get a chance			Publicly thank the person for going beyond what is normally expected		

Showing Innovation

3. When one of your direct reports demonstrates a new, better way of doing something that is a normal part of their job, you:

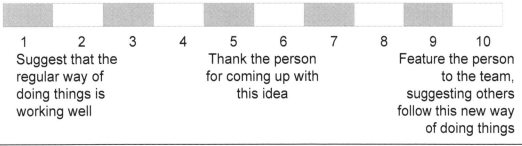

1	2	3	4	5	6	7	8	9	10
Suggest that the regular way of doing things is working well				Thank the person for coming up with this idea			Feature the person to the team, suggesting others follow this new way of doing things		

6. How do you performance contract for organization turnaround?

Over the last two years, at executive networking sessions, I have heard hundreds of executives describe themselves as being excellent at turnaround. As I listened, I realized that they were describing their process improvement skills, not their corporate turnaround abilities. They were talking about fixing up part of the whole, not turning around the whole organization when it was under threat.

One morning, as I was driving, I hear a professional house renovator - a "house re-newer" - describe he what did. He took care to distinguish what he did from folks who called themselves "renovators" but were really "part of a house" fixer-uppers.

> "When I renovate a place, the only things that will stay the same about the house are its external structure and its internal supporting walls. I pretty well gut everything else. When I am through, it's a very different place to live in. It is a much more effective and efficient house. It operates better as a home, and costs much less to run. It usually looks better from the outside as well, although everyone can still see that it is the same house."

What an insight! I immediately understood the difference between all those executives I have been listening to and corporate turnaround experts.

Process Improvers	Organization Renovators
Make improvements to 1 or more existing processes through improving automation or re-organizing work flow.	Address what needs to happen to ensure this organization survives and dramatically improves its results.

Process Improvers	Organization Renovators
	Figure out how to do it without destroying the organization (i.e. without tearing down "external and internal supporting walls" = destroying customer relationships or financial viability) while change is occurring.
Fit improvement into the "day to day" normal way of doing the other work in organization.	Tackle all processes in the organization and re-do them to achieve dramatic success. Do so a way that ensures that organization survives while undergoing whole scale internal change (i.e. the organization continues to serve customers, to provide services or make products, to pay its bills etc).
Help existing staff learn new improved processes	Challenge existing staff to come up to the new performance bench marks. Train them to do so if they are willing and if they can. If they don't, bring in people who do and fully integrate them into the team.
Fit the new ways of doing things into the existing culture of the organization.	Re-shape the culture, energizing the people. Get them to believe in their own personal future with the organization. More them from "react and get along" to "pro-act, create, provide services at extraordinary levels, achieve extraordinary results".

The metrics that are used in contracting with an executive for the improvement of existing process are straight forward. Processes do something. They produce output of some kind (e.g. service transactions, produces, units of information ….). They take energy to do (e.g. people hours, head count …).

To develop a process improvement metric, all you have to do is count the output and the input reliably. Put units of output over units of input and you have a useful "point in time" metric for that process. Add a relevant time period (e.g. days, or weeks, or months). Then watch the trend over time. When you do so, you have a clean, clear performance metric. Here are some classic examples:

- bank customers served per month / teller hours per month,

- bills paid per month / account payable staff hours,

- airline passenger miles per month / air crew hours per month,

- widgets produced per day / manufacturing staff hours per day.

Trend metrics such as these will tell you if the executive is "improving" the process.

You cannot take this approach when you contract with an organization renovation leader and his or her team. Every process inside the organization will be different by the time they through, just like the entire interior a house will be different by a true time house renovator is through.

Renovating an organization involves great urgency and wide-ranging change made under conditions of continuous organizational stress. Sometimes, part of the change goes backward for a time, in order for the whole change to go forward.

So how do you "measure" the performance success of an organization renovation leader and team? You need to take a much broader approach to metrics than when you are contracting for process improvement.

1. **Use metrics that look at the whole organization from the outside in.**

All kinds of process change will be happening in an organization during renovation. However, the overall pattern of positive change will be reflected in the trends in such "from outside the organization looking in" metrics.

An example is "$revenue produced / $dollar of operating expense" per month. Watch the trend. A downward slip for a month or two is expected. But a clear downward pattern that shows no sign of turnaround is not.

Using a number of them is better than using just one. When you do so, you can see if the general pattern is positive, even though one or two may be on a short term downward trend as change moves forward.

Add these whole organization metric trends to a "menu" of process improvement trend metrics that focus on specific internal process. An experienced organization renovation team uses both to monitor the impact of what they are doing both on specific processes, and on the whole organization.

2. **Expect the organization renovation leader and team to show how they are making both short term immediate changes and long term changes at the same time.**

Listen to them as they talk about this with you on a regular basis. If they cannot show how they are doing this, then this absence is in itself a "negative metric".

Ask for regular "review" sessions with the team. Expect the leader and the team to "insist" on having them. Expect them to initiate on the development of process improvement specific metrics that show what is happening as a result of their changes. Also expect them to develop and use relevant "outside the organization looking in" metrics to keep track of how the overall change is going.

An experienced organization renovation team is profoundly metrics based. They do not believe in the "power" of their personalities as the key to change. They do expect turbulence during the change. They have an integrated approach to change that both makes sense in the longer term and adapts to short term events as they move the organization renovation forward. Just like a house renovator, they take what they uncover into account as they make change.

3. **Expect negative trends in some of the process specific improvement metrics while you are seeing positive trends in others.**

The turbulence experienced during an organization renovation can means that things can look worse before they look better. Just imagine what the inside of a "renovated" house looks like before house renovators start building the new walls.

4. **Work with renovation team to identify the "supporting walls" for this organization – the key things that must continue to be in place while the change is happening.**

Develop metrics for each one. "Revenue per customer" and "customer satisfaction / engagement " are two examples for a customer service organization. Bringing revenue in is a "supporting wall" for such an organization, and is maintaining the customer's satisfaction level and engagement.

Watch the reaction of renovation leader and the team to any negative sustained trends in these metrics. They are about the organization's survival. Expect them to understand the importance of these metrics, and take negative trends in these key "survival" metrics extremely seriously. They need urgent corrective action.

Turning around an entire organization is very different from turning around a specific process within an organization. But you can still develop effective performance contracts for such total organization change. You just need to make sure that the performance metrics that you use reflect the totality of the change. You will know that you have the right turnaround leader and team when they are just as concerned about developing, monitoring and adjusting their work to a set of such metrics as you are.

7. How do you use performance contracting to pick "good", rather than "bad" organizational leaders?

"Why Are We Bad At Picking Good Leaders" (see the author's YouTube video at http://www.youtube.com/watch?v=hgHBFw8So2U) is 5th on Harvey Schachter's Toronto Globe and Mail Ten Best Business books of 2011.

In it, Jeffrey Cohn and Jay Moran present the 7 characteristics that they correlate with good leaders.

1. Integrity

2. Empathy

3. Emotional Intelligence

4. Vision

5. Judgment

6. Courage

7. Passion

These qualities have been praised by many other "leadership" writers over the years. Cohen and Moran tell organizations to select for organizational leaders who demonstrate these qualities. They provide "stories" which illustrate how they believe that organizations can do so.

But all of this advice may be missing an essential point. Finding a person who is exceptional on these 7 qualities may be a next to impossible task for most organizations.

Suppose that a "good" leader needs to demonstrate possession of all 7 qualities at a level that is at least 2 standard deviations above average. Simple math will shows that the likelihood of finding, i.e. selecting, such a person is very slight.

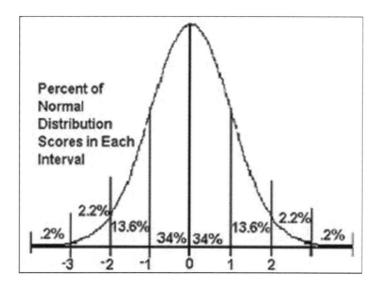

The normal distribution graph shows that only 2.4% (=2.2% + .2%) of the population will be 2 standard deviations above average when you consider 1 characteristic. If you expect an individual to be 2 standard deviations above average on 7 qualities, you have to multiply 2.4% by itself 7 times. If you do this on your calculator or in Excel, you will get a very small number indeed. The following table shows the probability of finding a person who is 2 standard deviations above average on a progressively greater number of qualities. As you can see as you want people to have such outstanding levels on more and more qualities, the less likely you are to find them.

# of Qualities	2 Standard Deviations above Average		1 Standard Deviations above Average	
	Cumulative Probability of Finding	# individuals in 1,000,000 people	Cumulative Probability of Finding	# individuals in 1,000,000 people
1	2.4%	24,000	16%	160,000
2	0.0576%	576	2.56%	25,600
3	0.0013824%	13.8	0.41%	4,096
4	0.0000332%	0.33	0.07%	655.4
5	0.0000008%	0.0080	0.0105%	104.9
6	0.00000002%	0.00019	0.00168%	16.8
7	0.0000000005%	0.0000046	0.00027%	2.7

Let's make it easier. Say that a good leader only needs to demonstrate these 7 qualities at a level that is 1 standard deviation above average. Even in this case, the chances of finding individuals who demonstrate all 7 of these qualities at this level are still pretty slim (2.7 people in each 1,000,000).

But we need to move beyond statistics. Cohn and Moran's 7 qualities are not "simple" human behaviors. They are human characteristics that depend on a complex interactive mix of genetics, up-bringing, experience and education. This is the reason why years of time and millions of dollars of organizational investment in "leadership" training and development have not really produced an abundance of "effective leaders" who posses these 7 qualities at these levels.

Does this mean that most organizations might as well forget the process of "finding" or "developing" good leaders? I don't believe so. What can an organization do find and to develop better leaders?

Organizations certainly need the succession planning processes that Cohn and Moran advocate. But organizations need to be base their decisions about individuals in such succession planning processes on an underlying performance management process that is strongly based on forward-looking, metric-based performance contracting.

An individual who consistently achieves or betters metric based performance targets over a number of years, in a variety of executive positions, is a potential future organizational leader. That person is demonstrating that she or he can apply the "right" personal characteristics to stand out from the average performer in "this" organization. Useful leadership is always demonstrated in the context of an specific organization's shifting specific economic, technological, social and cultural conditions over a number of years.

The abstract "leadership characteristic" labels (e.g. Integrity) used by Cohn and Moran, and many other writers on leadership, tend to ignore this. Executive search consultants and academic writers turn "leadership" into an abstraction precisely because they are removed from the day-to-day performance of people in their client organizations. They do not have to deal with leadership as a concrete set of behaviors demonstrated by a specific individual that lead to valued results in a specific organization over a significant period of time.

Executive search consultants perpetuate this tendency to relate "leading" to these kinds of highly abstract personal characteristics. It is a core assumption necessary to the continuation of their business. Unless clients believe that leadership is "transferable" from one organization to another, retained executive search for leaders from outside an organization makes no business sense.

If we approach "leading" in a less abstract way, and focus more on demonstrated "in context" performance, organizations are more likely to succeed at picking "good" leaders. Organizations that seriously want to "pick and develop" the leaders they need for the future will do the following.

1. Take care to develop their internal performance contracting competencies. They will use forward-looking personal performance contracts. These contracts will include a process by which boss and direct report contract to use metrics to track direct report performance delivery progress. These metrics will derive from the automated business applications the organization uses to track and to manage the work done on a day-to-day basis.

   Once such a forward looking contract is "signed" by both boss and direct report, these metrics will be delivered independently to both boss and direct report over the course of the performance period. As a result, the power relationship between them will shift. Bosses are more likely to become coaches when direct report performance goes off-track. Direct reports are more likely to "ask" for help when they see that they are under achieving.

2. Ensure that this performance contracting and progress monitoring process is in place for at least the "manager of others" levels and above in the organization.

3. Engage the senior most executives in systematically reviewing actual performance on such performance contracts by top performers: - individuals who consistently achieve and deliver at or beyond their contracted performance metrics.

4. Promote such top performing individuals so that over the years their job scope becomes more complex and wide ranging. As a result, maintaining "top performance" status will become harder and harder for such individuals over time. This will refine the identification of potential leaders based on actual performance, not personal loyalty or personality fit between boss and subordinate.

5. Move consistent top performing individuals to a variety of lateral assignments over the course of their career. This will allow the organization to see if their ability to deliver at or beyond contracted personal performance levels remains the same in a variety of organization environments (functional, operational and geographic).

"Picking good leaders" in this way will take commitment over a number of years. The performance contracts for the CEO and the CEO's immediate reports will require the presence of metrics that "show" that this is being well done.

Organizations that do this will not be "bad" at picking good leaders. Instead, they will be shaping their futures in way that increase their probability of long lasting competitive success over a number of executive generations.

8. Why I stopped doing performance appraisals and learned to implement performance contracting

How I Made the Decision to Stop

Over the course of my career, I have led teams of creative technical professionals, as well as whole organizations. Much of my executive work has been done in turnaround situations – either of an existing IT group or the whole organization.

Since my academic training includes work place psychology, I always have been intrigued by what academics and human resource professionals have had to say about performance appraisal. Early in my executive career, I followed the best practices in performance appraisal recommended by both groups. Performance management was a key tactic in my turn around and culture change work.

After a number of years, I realized that my experience with performance appraisal as an organization and culture change process left me feeling disappointed. Performance appraisal did not inspire people. It did not support my change process.

- I needed people to face our new future. Performance appraisal deals with the past.

- I needed people to commit to the results we needed to achieve. Performance appraisal told them, usually without clear performance evidence, how they had performed in the past.

The whole performance appraisal process seemed terribly subjective and power based.

I use employee satisfaction surveys as a culture change mechanism. Properly constructed and administered, such surveys monitor the effectiveness of my culture change efforts. I added questions about how staff saw performance appraisal as a result of my disappointment with it.

I quickly learned that the individuals who worked for me really disliked the performance appraisal process. Managers did not like doing them. Staff complained that they were arbitrary and de-motivating. Nobody felt that they actually helped people improve their performance.

I systematically reviewed the HR industry writing and academic research on performance appraisal. Mostly, it told me to try harder. It also told me annual performance appraisal without regular "through the year" meetings between manager and direct report was not likely to lead to performance improvement.

Based on this, I started to ask HR professionals in other organizations about their employee satisfaction survey findings about performance appraisal. I was able to tap into a research source that had confidential access to many such surveys. I found that people in most other organizations shared the frustrations of the managers and the staff who worked for me about performance appraisal.

So I asked myself:

- "Why did I continue to use a performance management process which de-motivates most people, the very opposite of what I am trying to achieve?

- "What management purposes did performance appraisal really serve?"

My answer to the first question was straight forward: stop doing performance appraisal and find a better way to motivate people to perform when doing organization turnarounds. I did. Eventually, I wrote about how I used performance contracting as an organizational change and organization renovation tool[6].

The answer to the second question were equally clear – in the research literature, in the HR industry press, and in what managers told me when I asked them. Here are some typical answers from managers that summarize my findings.

- "I need performance appraisal ratings to support the way in which I distribute yearend bonuses to my people."

- "By the time I finish the performance appraisals for my group, everyone is clear that I have the power as the boss to evaluate what they do. Performance appraisal re-enforces my authority over them, since it determines bonus payouts in our company."

- "HR keeps bugging me to get my performance appraisals done every year end. It is just something we do at year end. They collate the results for the whole

---

[6] See "Turning Around Organizations: A How To Guide" – Google it to find out how to get it.

organization and report them to the Board. But for the rest, performance appraisals don't seem to lead to any real results, even when we rate people as exceptional or as poor performers. It is just somewhat we have to do as managers."

Facilitating a Performance Level / Culture Fit Evaluation Process

At this point in my career, I took on the culture change leadership of a 1200 person organization of technical professionals. The existing culture was reactive, rather than proactive. The people were technology oriented rather than customer service oriented.

Performance management, based on the performance appraisal processes used in the rest of this major financial services corporation, had simply not been done for over 5 years. The argument presented by the previous management of this group was "We are too busy to waste time on performance appraisal".

The new leadership team did many things to turn around this organization. As culture change leader, I was responsible for re-vitalizing the performance management process. As well, I led the internal and external recruiting process that created a new management layer in this organization.

As individuals, and as a group, the members of this management team did not have valid insight into the talent and performance of the individuals in their teams. They needed a process that gave them "documented" insight into the caliber of these individuals. They needed to understand the fit of their team members to the new performance culture we were creating. The grid at the top of the following page summarizes these needs.

I designed, led and facilitated the difficult and contentious process that accomplished this. The process cascaded "up" in each working group in our IT organization. All the managers and directors from each IT sub-group, the vice-president involved, as well as appropriate managers from their "client and service groups", attended each working session.

HR professional staff attended as "documenters". They produced summary transcripts of the discussion about each individual and the placement of each person on the grid. These individual documents were signed by the managers involved in the dialogue. They became the replacement for the missing performance appraisal files for all of the individuals in this organization.

Evaluating Personal Performance and Future Culture Fit in A Turnaround Situation: The Process

The structure of the meetings

Each person in a manager's group was discussed in turn. We worked through all of the individuals who were direct reports to lowest level of manager in the room. When all of their direct reports have been discussed, this level of managers left the room.

		Fit to the culture we were creating	
		High	Low
Performance Delivery In the past two years	High	**Keep** = energize through performance contracting	**Save** = help make a transition to the new culture through performance contracting and personal development / coaching
	Low	**Review** = decide if we could get better performance by investing in a person's skill upgrade & delivery improvement Or Out Place	**Out Place** = move out of our IT organization as quickly as possible

The directors they reported to now went through the same process for the departed managers. This procedure cascaded up the reporting levels in the room until only the direct reports to the vice-president involved were left.

The direct reports to the vice-president level were discussed in a separate meeting of all of the vice-presidents. Appropriate key vice-presidents from the IT group's client organizations were involved in these discussions.

Evaluating individuals using behavioral evidence

1. The manager described "what the person in his or her team was responsible for". The other managers were polled to see if they agreed, or wanted to change elements of the responsibility description.

2. Once the "responsibility" for a person was agreed to, the manager talked about how the person's delivery on these responsibilities was to be measured. Other managers had to agree that they could "see" these metrics. Each metric were refined until it met this criteria.

3. The manager then presented a judgment about where the person's performance in the past two years fell on these metrics. On the basis of this, the person was assigned to the High or Low group on the performance axis of the grid on the previous page.

    Other managers, particularly managers from the client and service organizations, had to agree to and support this judgment. When they did not, the facilitator managed the discussion which resolved the difference in perceptions, and resulted in the person's final placement.

4. The discussion then shifted to the person's potential fit to the new culture. This dialogue started from a set of general criteria that was used in all of the meetings.

    - **High Fit** to our new culture = person's behaviour consistently demonstrated:

        ○ a concern about delivering results in a customer oriented way,

        ○ a willingness to accept and to act on metric based feedback on personal performance.

        ○ a willingness to learn new interpersonal skills if this was required to become a better team member and collaborator with others.

    - **Low fit** = person did not show behavioral evidence of the three High Fit criteria.

        To reduce the impact of "group think" on this process, each involved manager wrote down their personal rating of the individual being discussed before the dialogue started. These independently made judgments were disclosed as the first step, between any dialogue. Differences in judgments led to lengthy discussion. Agreement in perception was explored by asking the manager's involved to publicly state the reasons for their judgment.

Although this discussion was more subjective, the managers quickly learned that agreement among a relevant sub-set of the people in the room, who had substantial day-to-day contact with the individual being evaluated, led to "inter-subjective" objectivity.

5. Once the discussion was complete, the manager involved took a sticker with the evaluated person's name and placed it in the appropriate place on a wall version of the grid shown previously. The manager did this in front of peers and superiors. It turned the discussion into a public display of the manager's final judgment of the person. From a psychological point of view, this action turned a verbal dialogue into a personal whole body commitment in front of a group of relevant peers and superiors.

As the discussion progressed, this wall grid became a constant reminder of discussions that had gone on before. The dialogue about each current individual was in the "foreground" during the discussion of that person. The need to place this person on this wall at the end of the dialogue meant that the dialogue about the current person was constantly in relation to the "background" of all of the other people in the group. This foreground / background dynamic - taken from Gestalt psychology - increased the accuracy of the results.

The first dialogues about individuals took a long time in each new group. The managers were learning the process they needed to use in these first discussions. The facilitator strongly guided them on the process to use during these first evaluations.

The facilitator constantly challenged the managers to move from statements of "like or dislike" around the individuals to performance and metrics based judgments of their team members. The facilitator regularly noticed "non-verbal" indications of differing perceptions or disagreement in other managers in the room. The facilitator asked such individuals to provide their input if they did not speak up themselves.

Learning new skills important to the new culture

During these first dialogues, the managers learned how to use performance metrics to provide evidence of performance, something that had been missing in this organization. They learned to do this through acting under the guidance of the facilitator.

As the managers worked through their first disagreements in perception of the individual currently being discussed, they moved from feeling based conflict to resolving conflict through the presentation of evidence. Once again, this action based learning taught a skill badly lacking in this organization.

Finally, the managers learned that evidence based "inter-subjective" agreement was the key to being accurate in their evaluations of individuals. They learned to listen to others' perception of an individual. They could see the common elements in the

perceptions, and realize that agreement in perception across several people was often a more accurate picture of an individual working for them than their own.

As they acquired these skills, and as job based patterns of personal responsibility and metrics developed, each individual took less time to evaluate. The ability of the HR professionals to provide evidence from their transcripts of the ways in which previous versions of these patterns were resolved also reduced the time the group needed to effectively consider an individual. The presence of the "grid" on the wall, with its visual placement of the individuals who has already been discussed, allowed the managers relate elements relevant to the current individual under discussion to these re-occurring patterns.

Implementing Performance Contracting with the 'Keepers", "Savers", and "Reviewers"

When I designed this process, I anticipated the problems associated with changing the definition of peoples' roles (e.g. constructive dismissal) and out placement (e.g. wrongful termination).

The HR group in this organization developed an effective out placement program for the people in the Low Performance – Low Cultural Fit = Out Place box. Not a single individual (there were several hundred) challenged their outplacement.

1. The settlement packages were reasonable, and conformed to current precedents set by the courts.

   The cost of these packages, although considerable, was low compared to the benefits **obtained through tremendous upsurge in productivity** that occurred in this organization as soon as these "Low-Low" people were gone. The departed were no longer a "drag" on this organization.

2. These technical people support the overall productivity of a multi-billion dollar organization through the services they delivered. The dramatic increase in service delivery by the remaining IT staff put many times the cost of the outplacement program on the bottom line.

3. The evaluation process was very accurate. Socially, every person who remained in this IT organization knew that that this process had identified the actual non-performers in the organization. As a result, they supported the outplacements.

As part of our positive work with the "Keepers, Savers and Reviewers", we focused on what they were to do in the coming months. Managers sat down with the "Keepers, Savers and Reviewers" and talked about what they were supposed to do. They "negotiated" performance goals with them. They also negotiated the metrics that would be used to evaluate each person's upcoming results delivery. They succeed at this because of new skills they had acquired during the evaluation process. Performance contracting was a natural extension of this group validated individual evaluation process.

Most of the low performers who did fit our new forward-looking, customer-oriented, and metrics-using culture simply stopped being low performers. They liked the fact that they could "self-evaluate" their own performance over the year based on the metrics in their performance contracts. When they had problems delivering, they asked either their manager or their peers for help to fix the issue.

Of course, there were a few problem folks. Most of them came to the conclusion that our new culture was not for them, and left of their own accord.

We did have to take a "out placement" steps with a very few individuals over the next year or so. Doing so was quite straight forward. The individual had agreed to the metrics in the personal performance contract. The fact that the person was not delivering to the level contracted could not be disputed. The factual evidence collected to populate these metrics was straight forward. These facts could not be denied. As a result, managers could directly address the need for these individuals to improve their performance. HR based support resources helped managers to prepare for this manager – low performer problem solving.

Their performance of these individuals either improved, or they came to the realization that they needed to leave.

I have never done a performance appraisal since this experience. I simply don't believe performance appraisal is useful for motivating individuals to perform. That's why my slogan for performance contracting is:

Shape the Future, Don't Appraise the Past.™

Section Two

Avoiding Bad Hires:
The Steep Cost of Hiring Mistakes

WeCRUT3.com helps clients find the talent they need to succeed.

"Performance Based Recruiting:
Give us your recruiting muck and gluck,
we will give you back 3 final candidates,
for a great price."

The Hire for Performance Framework

WeCrut3.com's Hiring Results Framework

	LOW	MEDIUM	HIGH
EXCEEDS	BAD HIRE: IMMEDIATE DISCONNECT BETWEEN HIRED PERSON AND OTHERS	SOME CONNECTION BETWEEN HIRED PERSON AND OTHERS, BUT INDIVIDUAL WILL BE FRUSTRATED BY PERFORMANCE DEMANDS OF JOB	GOOD CONNECTION BETWEEN HIRED PERSON AND OTHERS – BUT LONG TERM TROUBLE UNLESS JOB CONTENT UPGRADED
HIGH	HIRED PERSON CAN DO JOB, BUT WILL NOT "ENJOY" WORKING WITH OTHERS – WORKS FOR ISOLATED INDIVIDUAL CONTRIBUTORS ONLY	HIRED PERSON WILL DO JOB, BUT IN THE LONGER RUN, COULD BE GROWING DISCONNECT BETWEEN PERSON AND CO-WORKERS	GREAT FIT ON BOTH PERFORMANCE AND CULTURE
MEDIUM	POOR FIT WITH COWORKERS AND LESS THAT REQUIRED PERFORMANCE – EASIER TO "LET GO"	HIRED PERSON WILL NOT PERFORM AS REQUIRED, AND THERE COULD BE GROWING DISCONNECT BETWEEN PERSON AND CO-WORKERS	HIRED PERSON WILL BE LIKED AND FIT IN WITH OTHERS BUT NOT PERFORM AS REQUIRED: DIFFICULT TO "LET GO"
LOW	DO NOT HIRE: IF HIRED, END EMPLOYMENT ASAP	BAD HIRE: END EMPLOYMENT AS SOON AS POSSIBLE	BAD HIRE: POOR PERFORMANCE BUT FIT BETWEEN PERSON AND CO-WORKERS MAKES IT DIFFICULT TO DEAL STRAIGHT FORWARDLY

Fit between the Capability of the Candidate And the Technical Performance Requirements of the Job (vertical axis)

Fit between Personality of the Candidate And the Culture of the Organization (horizontal axis)

"Great personal performance means that
you have to hire for both
performance fit and culture fit.
Bad hires cost.
Avoiding bad hires is one
of the most important ways
in which your organization can
save money, increase morale and achieve excellence."

A Bad Hire = Poor Performance Fit and / or Poor Culture Fit

The Cost of a Hiring Mistake

Today it is well accepted that hiring mistakes cost organizations real money. May people think that is the smallest part of the problem. Some experts estimate the cost of a bad hire can be 3 to 5 times the original salary. Lost productivity, negative impact on morale and distraction from the core work of the organization can be soft costs which are far more detrimental than the dollars lost to the organization.

Avoiding hiring mistakes simply makes sense. But doing so is not always easy. Recruiters, whenever internal or external[7], and hiring managers, need to take a number of steps that go beyond the resume review and face to face interviewing approach that makes up the core of today's recruiting practice.

A Bad Hire = Poor Performance Fit and / or Poor Culture Fit

A candidate's actual performance on-the-job results from two kinds of "fit". The first has to do with the fit between a candidate's capability – the person's skills and experience - and the performance requirements of the job. The second has to do with the fit between the candidate's personality and the culture of the organization. Lack of fit on either, or on both, can lead to a bad hire

Predicting Performance Fit

Recruiters can assess a candidate's performance fit. But to do so, they must really understand the job, not in the abstract, but concretely. Recruiters need a clear sense of what the new hire will be doing in the first 3 months and in the first year. They do not need to be able to do these things, or even manage them. But that may take technical skills they do not have. But they do need to know what it is like to manage performance. That is why the best recruiters are former managers who have turned to recruiting, not individuals who have done nothing but recruit during their careers.

Recruiters who accurately predict on-the-job performance consistently do three things.

1. They work with the hiring manager to develop **a performance map** that clarifies what a new hire is expected to do in the first 3 months, and in the first year on-the-job.

2. They get early **candidates to behave - to do thing other than respond to interview questions - as early as possible** in the recruiting cycle.

---

[7] Everything that follows applies equally to internal or external recruiters. The way in which things are done might be slightly different. The need to do these things is not.

3. They create events that **require final candidates to demonstrate what they can to the hiring manager and future work peers.**

Let's look at each of these three recruiter behaviors in more detail.

Creating and Using Performance Maps During Recruiting

When recruiters work with a hiring manager to create a performance map, they do the following.

1. Recruiters translate the hiring manager's general expectations about what the new hire will do into 3 to 7[8] clear things that the new hire will need to do or get done through others e.g. direct reports.. (**S**pecific and concrete)

2. Recruiters dialogue with the hiring manager till each of these specific performance items has a defined measure. Essentially, this measure answers the following questions: (**M**easureable) .

   ◦ What will, I the hiring manager, see and hear when this item is completed or this objective is achieved?

   ◦ What signs, signals, metrics will I, the hiring manager, use to evaluate the "degree of quality or completion"?. How will I use them?

3. Recruiters clarify the "authority" the new hire will have over resources (dollar, people, facilities), so that it is clear that the person will be actually be able to do what is needed to achieve the objective (**A**ctionable).

4. Recruiters ensure that each objective specifies the things that will be produced as a result of the work that is done (**R**esults Based).

5. Recruiters get the hiring manager to indicate the time frame in which the delivery is expected (**T**ime frame).

6. Recruiters place the objective into the organizational context in which the new hire will have to do what it gets to deliver against the performance expectation (**E**nvironment).[9]

---

[8] **"The Magical Number Seven, Plus or Minus Two: Some Limits on Our Capacity for Processing Information"** is one of the most highly cited papers in psychology It was published in 1956 by the cognitive psychologist George A. Miller of Princeton University's Department of Psychology in *Psychological Review*. It is often interpreted to argue that the number of objects an average human can hold in working memory is 7 ± 2. This is frequently referred to as *Miller's Law*. See the Wikipedia article at http://en.wikipedia.org/wiki/The_Magical_Number_Seven,_Plus_or_Minus_Two.

For senior positions, 3 to 7 items may not be enough. The complexity of the job requires more. When this is the case, it is best to organize them into a hierarchy of items and sub-items, where each level contains the no more than 3 to 7 items.

In organizations which use performance appraisal to manage performance, hiring managers often don't do this kind of "before the fact" thinking about performance. They are used to, and rewarded for, to doing "looking back" evaluation[10] of performance in traditional performance appraisals[11].

In such situations, the recruiter needs to inspire the manager to engage in this process. Once of the best ways of doing this by taking the manager through a well structured dialogue which helps clarify these forward looking performance expectations. The recruiter writes up the information obtained in a "performance map" format that is useful to both.

The recruiter uses the map to screen candidates. Recruiters, especially recruiters who have managed people during their own past careers, gain a clear picture of the job that the final hire will need to do when they prepare performance maps. As a result, recruiters who use performance maps can recruit for many different types of positions. They do not need to become narrow recruiting specialists (e.g. an IT recruiter, or a finance recruiter and so on …). The combination of the performance map and their managerial experience allows them to understand what need to be done many jobs, rather than just a few. They do not have to guess and "mind read" the job requirements. By talking with the hiring manager they know. When they engage in this process, they also build the trust with the hiring manager which is essential to their joint recruiting success.

The manager uses the performance map in the final candidate interview process to engage in a deeper dialogue than normally occurs in job interview. With a clear forward looking performance map, the manager can ask "how would you go about doing this" probes which provide insight into the way in which the candidate is likely to behave in this job. As the person talks about these hows, the manager can ask follow up probes that make sure that the individual "grounds" what they are saying.

---

[9] The idea of SMART objective (specific and concrete, measureable, actionable, results driven and timed) has been around for a long time. Adding the environment – the organizational context – turns SMART into SMARTE. But it also adds an important element that is often taken for granted by hiring decision makers, and never taken for granted by the best candidates. They want to know it, since it is an important part of what they consider when deciding whether or not to take a new job.

[10] In 1999, Marcus Buckingham and Curt Coffman of the Gallup Group wrote First Break All the Rules: What the World's Greatest Managers Do Differently". This is where they first introduced their list of criteria that employees require in order to maximize their performance and on-the-job satisfaction. At the top of the list were: clarifying expectations up front, providing people with the right tools and resources to do the job properly, having managers that support them, and being assigned work they enjoy and are good at.
(see http://businessjournal.gallup.com/content/1144/First-Break-All-Rules-Book-Center.aspx)

[11] There is a lot of evidence, both research based and anecdotal, that organization members find the traditional performance appraisal process confusing, demoralizing and un-motivating See the Wikipedia article on performance appraisal to learn more about performance appraisal and its current state of practice. http://en.wikipedia.org/wiki/Performance_appraisal

Some interviewees mentally quick on their feet. They can make up reasonable answers to how would you do this questions. When the hiring manager follows up with a "give me an example of when and how you have done something similar to this in your past", this becomes apparent. Thoughtful probing of this kind will quickly make it clear if the individual is simply verbally clever in an interview, or has actual relevant experience which can be applied in this job.

1. The Extra Benefits to Starting with A Performance Map

The performance map also acts as a "on-boarding" framework. Getting new hires productive quickly is essential. Once a new hire comes on board, the hiring manager can use the performance map to clearly convey what is required in the first 3 months, and in the first year.

For the new hire, the performance map acts as a guide to "what do I need to learn about this place, who do I need to interact with, and what do I need to do". As a result, new hires are not confused about their new roles from day 1.

Dialogue between the new hire and manager can modify detail out any of the elements recruiting performance map. Circumstances change. The two individuals are getting to know one another by working together. The recruiting performance map acts as a focusing device. It provides a structure for the first working dialogues between then. Once they start to work in this way, they are highly likely to continue it. In this way, a recruiting performance map sets up This a relationship between manager and new hire that is performance contracting based.

2. Getting the Candidates to Behave Early in the Recruiting Process

Experienced managers know that the single best predictor of future behavior on the part of a direct report is current behavior. That is why managers coach and make investments in professional development. They know that it takes a "distancing event" like coaching or training to help the direct report bridge from old patterns of behavior to new ones.

The same thing holds true for candidates. Recruiters who focus completely on candidates past behavior, e.g. through a review of the resume, get access to only a limited spectrum of current candidate's behavior – their behavior as interviewees.

Just a few minutes with Google will convince anyone that there is lots of "good training" in on how to handle a recruiting interview available to candidates for free. Good candidates take recruiting interviews seriously. They research the organization. They rehearse their responses to likely interview questions. As a result, the only thing that a recruiter can reliably predict based on a candidate's interview behavior is how well that person will behave in a future recruiting interview[12].

But recruiters don't need to limit themselves to resume review type questioning. They can create scenarios and question sets that get candidates to "do", to perform tasks relevant to their future on-the-job performance. The performance map is key. Based on it, a recruiter can craft these type of questions.

With the Internet, it is even possible to get potential candidates to submit such "samples of doing" along with their resumes and cover letters. The wide spread availability of the cell phone cameras and web cams will continue to change recruiting practice. Recruiters have a choice. Do so wisely based on performance maps, which lead to very job relevant questions. Or do so based on stereotypical ideas of what "candidates" should say in these kinds of submissions. The sooner recruiters embed this type of "show me what you can do" events, based on immediately relevant performance maps, in the candidate review work flow, the better the quality of final candidates will be.

3. Creating Events that Allow Final Candidates to Show What They Can Do

Final candidates need to do more than just talk. By the time, the recruitment is down to the 2 or 3 people who could potential receive a job offer, the stakes are higher, both for the hiring organization and the candidate. They need to behave in ways that approximate some of the ways in which they will behave in the work place. Both sides need more in-depth information on which to make a final decision. The recruiter must stake "hiring" events that allows both sides to get this information.

These events need not be elaborate. Ten minutes of candidate behavior, followed by 10 to 20 minutes of interaction with 3 to 5 people, can provide a great deal of insight into how a person will behave on-the-job. But the event needs to be relevant. Its framing and the follow up that happens after it need to be disciplined and systematic. Here are some examples of relevant events.

1. The candidate is asked to behave in a way that is quite close to one of the ways that the person will have to behave on-the-job.

    Examples:
    ▪   make a short Power Point presentation that deals with one of the items in the Performance Map,

    ▪   show and demonstrate the result of a piece of work that you have done recently that could be part of this new job,

---

[12] Even behavioral interviewing, once thought to be the best way to interview candidates, is subject to this. See this "teaching site" for job candidates at the University of Washington as an example http://www.washington.edu/admin/hr/roles/mgr/hire/interview-select/behavioral.html

- analyze a short case that comes from the new job environment and show how you would act in response to it,

- participate in a role play simulation of a typical customer interaction.

The possibilities are endless.

2. Following the final candidate piece, there is a short period of interaction among the final candidate, hiring managers and 3 to 5 potential co-workers. These folks asks questions and engage in dialogue with final candidate.

3. The recruiter engages these each of the individuals in the hiring organization one by one right after the event. The recruiter collects their independent impressions of the final candidate. As well, the recruiter asks each of them to independently rate of their perception of the candidate's: A simple version of this form follows.

Performance Fit

How well do you think or feel this person will be able to carry out the work / the duties in this position?

Not at all   **Very Well**

1	2	3	4	5	6	7	8	9	10

The results are collected and placed on a pictograph which visually presents what people thought.

Candidate: **E. Sample**
Position: **Sample Position**
Summary of Performance Fit Ratings

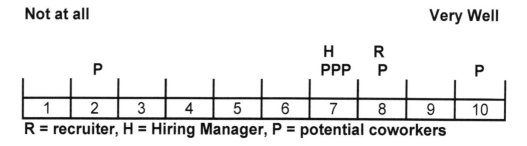

Once the picture is complete, the recruiter can explore any obvious differences. For example, in the pictograph above, the recruiter will contact the person who rate the final candidate two and get a clear idea of what lies behind their rating.

Predicting Culture Fit

The interaction between the final candidates and these folks after these events also provides sufficient data to all these people to predict the final candidate's degree of culture fit. The important thing to remember about culture is that it is a living thing that exists only in the moment – in the actual behavior of the people in the organization. It is the "walk" that happens each and every day in the organization. It is the way that people relate to one another. It is what they expect of one another and how they respond to others' expectations of them. It reflects what the organization is doing, the assets it is using to do those things, the industry or part of society in which the organization is positioned, the personality and the examples set by the behaviour of the organization's leaders.

Predicting a final candidate's cultural fit requires techniques that accept this reality. Skilled, experienced recruiters can make good intuitive guesses about a final candidate's likely culture fit. But they cannot really assess it accurately. Neither can hiring managers. However, both can contribute to the process which does do an effective cultural fit assessment.

The only practical way to get a solid reading on the extent to which an final candidate fits into an organization culture is to shape a set of event in which the candidate interacts with a number of the people from the organization. Using a structured process, each of these people is asked to make a subjective, independent assessment of the degree to which the candidate fits the culture AFTER they have interacted with the final candidate at this event. The judgment is entirely subjective. They don't need to explain it. They simply need to make it.

The recruiter can ask for this at the same time as the individuals rate a final candidate's Performance Fit. Once again, using a structured form that asks the question to each of the people in the same way is important. It is also important to ensure that they make these judgments independently. The recruiter needs to caution them not to talk to one another about this final candidate until this process is complete.

Culture Fit

How well do you think or feel this person will fit into our organization and get along with us as we work together?

Not at all   **Very Well**

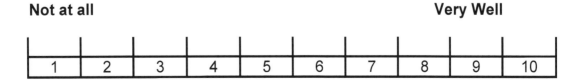

These independent assessments are collected and profiled visually. The resulting pattern is an effective predictor of the degree of a final candidate's cultural fit[13].

Candidate: **E. Sample**
Position: **Sample Position**
Summary of Culture Fit Ratings

Not at all   **Very Well**

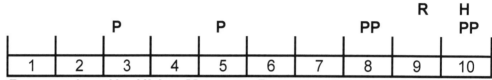

R = recruiter, H = Hiring Manager, P = potential coworkers

---

[13] This process adapts the Delphi technique to assessing / predicting cultural fit. It treats the people in an organization as "experts" about the culture. It uses structured data collection of independent judgments based on interpersonal interaction in "day to day work like events". When done in this way, it is a solid way to predict degree of culture fit. See http://en.wikipedia.org/wiki/Delphi_method for more on the Delphi forecasting technique.

Using the Hiring Results Framework to Understand Candidate Fit

The Hiring Results Framework

The two kinds of "fit" interact. The schematic below illustrates this. The fit between the performance requirements of the position and a candidate's capability have been placed on the vertical axis. The large number of degree of fit possibilities on this scale has been simplified to four - Low, Medium, High, and Exceeds. The last two cover the situations in which a candidate has more skill and experience than needed to handle the performance requirements of the job.

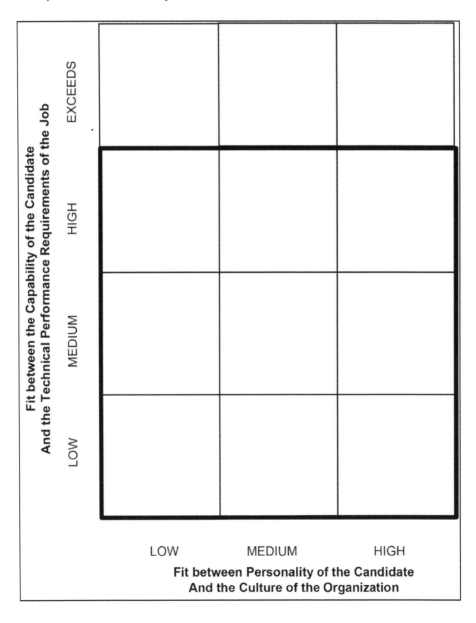

The fit between a candidate's personality and the organization's culture is shown on the horizontal axis. Degree of fit on this axis has simplified to three levels - Low, Medium, and High.

This leads to twelve possible hiring result scenarios. Nine of these, the ones in the lower part of the schematic, occur as part of most organization's normal hiring process. The remaining three, the ones at the top of the schematic, occur when recruiters and hiring managers deliberately over-hire on performance fit.

Over Hiring For Performance

Recruiters and hiring managers sometimes hire people who are clearly over-qualified for the day-to-day performance requirements of the job. Individuals who are dramatically over qualified are usually the issue. Their past earning levels are high enough to remove them from consideration.

	EXCEEDS		
	BAD HIRE: IMMEDIATE DISCONNECT BETWEEN HIRED PERSON AND OTHERS	SOME CONNECTION BETWEEN HIRED PERSON AND OTHERS, BUT INDIVIDUAL WILL BE FRUSTRATED BY PERFORMANCE DEMANDS OF JOB	GOOD CONNECTION BETWEEN HIRED PERSON AND OTHERS – BUT LONG TERM TROUBLE UNLESS JOB CONTENT UPGRADED
	LOW	MEDIUM	HIGH

**Fit between Personality of the Candidate
And the Culture of the Organization**

"Somewhat" over qualified individuals are whose personal capability exceeds the job performance requirements, but whose career and earning history still makes them "potential" candidates. . Recruiters and hiring managers often believe that "some over qualification" is a bit of a safety value. They will often hire such people when they believe that the work group the individual will join is under some degree of performance pressure.

Unless the organization is capable of dealing quickly with the frustration such hired people feel once they are one the job, such hires inevitably become problematic ones. The depth of the future problem with such hires is a function of the fit between the over qualified individual's personality and the culture of the work group.

Over hiring on performance only makes sense when the organization is growing dramatically. In such organizations, managers can rapidly upgrade job content, creating

appropriate fit between the person's capability and performance requirements of the job. If the culture is strongly oriented to promoting on the basis of merit, such individuals can also quickly be moved into more demanding positions.

This coping tactic works best when there is a high degree of fit between the candidate's personality and the culture. If there is not, job content upgrading or promotion at best delay the onset of the problems associated with the type of problematic hire. Sometimes, the problem is solved when the hired individual simply leaves, often shortly after taking the job. The organization simply experiences the cost of finding another person.

More serious impacts occur when the hired person stays and starts to express personal frustration to co-workers. As a result, co-workers may distance themselves from that individual, resulting in decreased productively and bad feelings in the work group. Alternatively, the frustration being expressed by the hired person may lead co-workers to develop negative perceptions about the organization. Once again, productivity suffers.

Hiring High Performance Fit Individuals

When the individual capability to job performance required fit is high, the degree of culture fit makes the difference between great hires and problematic ones.

Low alignment between the person's personality and the culture means that the individual will not enjoy working in this organization. If the job is that of an individual contributor, who has little to no interaction with other co-workers, this may not matter. But there are few such jobs. Productivity normally depends on people working with one another. If the interaction goes smoothly, aligning well with the living culture of the organization, everyone involved will feel comfortable with the interaction. There will be no negative impact on productivity. If there is some level of discomfort, some disconnect between the hired person and the others in the organization in their day-to-day interaction, productivity will be negatively impacted.

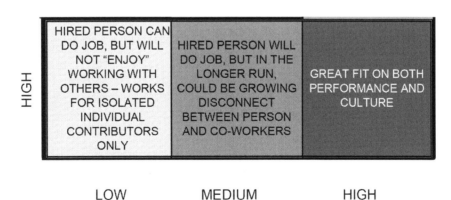

**Fit between Personality of the Candidate
And the Culture of the Organization**

When the performance fit is high, and the culture fit is medium, this may not be an immediate problem. The hired person could be reasonably productive for a long period of time (months to years). Outside factors could impact the work group in this time period, leading to adaptive changes in the day to day culture that align the person and the others in the work group. The personality of the hired person could be such that there is a positive impact on the work group day to day behavior. As a result, underlying initial cultural fit dynamic could disappear, or never be an issue.

In fact, organizations sometimes hire individuals who they hope will produce desired changes in the culture. They are explicitly depending upon these dynamics. There needs to be some level of fit between the personality of the hired person and the current culture. Without it, the potential of early disconnect is so high that the new person cannot have a positive impact on co-workers. Effective change agents and executives have this ability. They know how to behave in ways which demonstrate that they are "somewhat aligned with the current culture". This allows them to develop an initial level of rapport with others in the organization. When this reaches a level sufficient to start the cultural change moving forward, they start to introduce the factors that produce change in the culture. Based on their first successes, they progressively introduce more and more cultural change.

Six Types of Problematic Hires and their Potential Consequences

The remaining six possibilities are all problematic. The color in each cells below conveys two things. First, darker colors indicate the degree of negative impact on productivity. Secondly, darker colors indicate the degree of difficulty that organizations experience in dealing with these bad" hires.

Medium and Low performance fit is usually apparent in the first weeks and months that a hired individual is in the job. When culture fit is low, organizations normally have little difficulty handling these cases. Properly written probation period clauses in offer letters allow most organizations to simply terminate the individual. The organization merely incurs a rehiring cost. Financial pressures may lead hiring managers not to take this step. This inevitably ends up costing more in lost productivity and other indirect costs than the cost of a better re-hire.

When culture fit is medium, things get more complicated. The medium or low level of performance on the part of the hired individual gets "clouded" by the fact the individual is getting along on some level with co-workers (including the hiring manager). People have a natural reluctance to take what they perceive as negative with regard to a person with whom they are getting along. As a result, the probation period often concludes with no action. Once the probation period is over, dealing with the performance issues becomes more complicated and difficult.

MEDIUM	POOR FIT WITH COWORKERS AND LESS THAT REQUIRED PERFORMANCE – EASIER TO "LET GO"	HIRED PERSON WILL NOT PERFORM AS REQUIRED, AND THERE COULD BE GROWING DISCONNECT BETWEEN PERSON AND CO-WORKERS	HIRED PERSON WILL BE LIKED AND FIT IN WITH OTHERS BUT NOT PERFORM AS REQUIRED: DIFFICULT TO "LET GO"
LOW	DO NOT HIRE: IF HIRED, END EMPLOYMENT ASAP	BAD HIRE: END EMPLOYMENT AS SOON AS POSSIBLE	BAD HIRE: POOR PERFORMANCE BUT FIT BETWEEN PERSON AND CO-WORKERS MAKES IT DIFFICULT TO DEAL STRAIGHT FORWARDLY
	LOW	MEDIUM	HIGH

**Fit between Personality of the Candidate
And the Culture of the Organization**

This dynamic is much stronger when there is a high degree of fit between the personality of the hired individual and the culture of the organization. The person "fits in" even though the person's performance may not be what is required.

In either case, dealing with the performance problem is no longer straightforward. The hiring manager or the co-workers may make an effort to "train" the person, formally or informally. Sometimes this works, often it does not. The manager will use the organization's performance management to put the person on notice about their lack of performance. Often, this means dealing with this over several performance appraisal cycles. The feelings produced by this are not pleasant for either the manager or the person. The individual may leave, often to the relief of the manager and the co-workers. Sometimes, managers find it "easier" to avoid these unpleasant feelings and move the person to another part of the organization, through transfer or promotion. It solves the immediate work group's problem, but usually recreates the issue somewhere else in the organization. In fact, it can extend it to impact more people when the movement mechanism is promotion.

Hire Appropriately – But How … …

Good hires mean that both performance fit and culture fit are high. How do recruiters and hiring managers need to behave in order to do this?

First, recruiters and hiring managers must accept the following things.

1. The first is that they must separate the assessment of candidates into two clear parts. The assessment of a person's capability to job performance fit must be cleanly split from the assessment of a person's personality to culture fit.

2. The second is that the three most used hiring techniques:

   ◦ key word based resume ranking,
   ◦ recruiter and hiring manager personal review of highly ranked resumes,
   ◦ and face-to-face interviewing in which recruiters probe about past on-the-job performance based on what is written on the resume,

   are **not effective predictors of either future on-the-job performance or of culture fit.**

   The reasons for this are clear and well understood by job search researchers, if not by all recruiting professionals and hiring managers.

   More and more, resumes today are structured to take advantage of Internet job board key word search algorithms. Often, they are written by professional resume writers, who are fully aware of how to "lace" resume text with the key words that will result in a resume being highly ranked by such algorithms. As a result, especially in a world where job boards receive hundreds of resumes in response to a job advertisement, the algorithms used by job boards are not as effective at top ranking the best candidates as they once were

   For years, well structured research has clearly shown that there is a low relationship between candidates' interview behavior and their eventual performance on-the-job. Candidates may have far better "interview skills" than they have on-the-job skills.

   Most recruiters and hiring managers still depend upon unstructured one-on-one interviews as their prime candidate evaluation technique. Despite decades of formal training in recruiter skills such as behavioral interviewing, research continues to show that recruiters' and hiring managers' interview based ranking of candidates is a poor predictor of actual on-the-job performance[14].

3. The fact that organizations continue to rely upon interviewing as their prime assessment technique is probably the result of human evolution. As human beings,

---

[14] See http://www.ere.net/2011/09/27/why-interviews-are-a-waste-of-time/ for an informed practitioner's opinion "Why Interviews are A Waste of Time?"
See
http://mavweb.mnsu.edu/howard/Schmidt%20and%20Hunter%201998%20Validity%20and%20Utility%20Psychological%20Bulletin.pdf for an academic review "The Validity and Utility of Selection Methods in Personnel Psychology: Practical and Theoretical Implications of 85 Years of Research Findings" by Frank L. Schmidt and John E. Hunter, Psychological Bulletin, 1998, Volume 124, Number 2.

we have evolved to be instant evaluators of others, based on our first total impression of the other person, nonverbal and verbal. Sandy Pentland of MIT has led a sophisticated research program which clearly demonstrates this. His book "Honest Signals[15]" makes fascinating reading. But the ability to make quick first impressions about a stranger met in the bush or in the field is not a sound skill on which to base hiring decisions. Nevertheless, it is an instinctive skill which is deeply wired into our brains. We tend to rely on these skills, even when the situation in which we apply them (hiring candidates) is very different from the situations in which they evolved (surviving with meeting strangers in the bush or on the veldt).

Recruiters and Hiring Managers

Many recruiters tell tales of how their efforts to take these findings into account are undermined by the reluctance of hiring mangers to move beyond their intuitive belief that they are effective hirers. Attempts to use candidate behavior assessment and group / final candidate meeting techniques are often dismissed by hiring managers. When appropriately done, both of these techniques are much more effective predictors of performance fit and cultural fit than recruiter/hiring manager interviews.

Since they see themselves, not the HR professionals, as having the ultimate responsibility for on-the-job performance, hiring managers will often undermine the efforts of HR professionals to improve the hiring process. "I don't have the time": and "Just get me the resumes, and I will know who I want to see" are the two most common responses that hiring mangers make to HR suggestions to use more effective candidate assessment techniques. Prepared interview outlines, short presentations by final candidates to potential co-workers, working problem solving sessions with potential co-workers, review of past "work" submitted by candidates (candidate portfolios0, multiple peer interviews, systematic use of rating forms by all interviewers are all techniques that work.

Often such techniques are used by "excellent organizations". They become "lionized" by the trade press, show up in conference presentations, and are well publicized on the Internet. South West Airlines' use of structured candidate group interviews for cabin crew and Google's use of multiple peer interviews for professional staff are two such examples.

But this has little impact on the opinions of the majority of hiring managers in many organizations. They know that they are "excellent" interviewers. Their opinions override the reality of data. Unless there is explicit direction from the highest levels of the organization they will fall back on what they know to work. As Sandy Pentland has convincingly shown, it does work, in social situations, when immediate assessment of possibility of safe interaction with a newly met stranger in the next 5 to 90 minutes, is what is needed. But that is not the same thing as predicting future on-the-job

---

[15] Go to http://web.media.mit.edu/~sandy/ to see more about Alex "Sandy" Pentland and his work.

performance for a number of months and years based on a 60 to 90 minute face to face interview.

The Better Way, Even if it is Not the Most Commonly Adopted Way

Resume and face-to-face interviews continue to have a place in hiring. But they must be used differently if organizations desire to consistently avoid the 11 problematic hiring scenarios.

All of these better ways require that the recruiting process assess current candidate work place, not interview, behavior in order to predict on-the-job performance and culture fit. There are many ways of doing so. A complete description of the techniques, and the best way of employing them, is the appropriate topic of books. The following hiring case history illustrates some of them.

Widget's Recruiting Process for Professional Staff

Janine, in the HR group at Widget Corporation, is asked to recruit two design engineers

Janine, the senior recruiter in HR at Widget Corporation, has been approached by Maxwell, a lead engineer in Widget's product design group to do a recruitment for two new design engineers. Maxwell has asked Janine to get him some relevant resumes. He has told her that he will know the right candidates when he sees 20 or so resumes. He will then select 2 or 3 people to interview. Based on that, he will know the "right one" to hire.

Janine gently but persistently informs him that that is not how hiring is done at Widget. She gives him an outline of the steps normally used. Janine informs him that Maxine Bridot, Widget's CEO, has made a 15 minute video presentation on how hiring mistakes hurt Widget's competitive ability in the market place. She gives him the CD and asks him to view it as soon as possible.

Janine knows that Maxine will stress that it is responsibility of the Widget recruiter to avoid and to rectify hiring mistakes. She also knows that Maxine will clarify that this is not the same thing as being responsible for post probation on-the-job performance, which is the manager's responsibility.

Janine realizes that her work as a recruiter involves much more than simply interviewing candidates. Her recruiting case load, and the training she has received, reflects this reality. Her personal performance contract metrics mean that a single hiring mistake for which she was recruiter which is not rectified within the probation period will mean the loss of her annual performance bonus.

To give her the authority she needs to be able to address such mistakes, any newly hired individual is not finally transferred to the hiring manager's personnel authority until the end of the probation period. This is normally 70 working days after the person's start date. Before that date, Janine has full performance assessment authority over the individual. She can initiate the dismissal of the individual even if the hiring manager is unhappy about this. Although she has this authority, she also knows that a regular pattern of doing so will be viewed a lack of recruiting competence on her part by her own boss. Janine starts the steps in the recruitment process.

Performance Maps, not Job Descriptions

1. Janine pulls and reviews existing performance contracts for similar positions. No specific performance contract exists for these two new positions. So Janine will have to create a performance map from scratch, rather than develop one from existing performance contracts.

2. Janine will interview Maxwell, the hiring manager involved about the job, and prepare a short performance map. The performance map is not a job description[16]. Instead, it is a set of 3 to 7[17] performance objectives, set out in a way that meets the SMARTE[18] framework, that describes with a the new hire is expected to do in the first 3 months and the first year.

---

[16] What is the difference between a Job Description, a Performance Map, and a Role Accountability Map?

A Job Description describes the main tasks or activities that make up a job. It may or may not include information on the skills, experience or competency required to do these task or activities. Job descriptions lead to "what skills do you have or have you demonstrated in the past" type questions in recruiting.

A performance map lays out the accountabilities – the things a job or role is responsible for, as well as the metrics which will be used to measure whether or not those accountabilities are achieved. It is performance oriented, looks ahead, and does not focus on skill or competencies. Instead, it leads to the questions about "how will you behave to achieve these accountabilities and deliver the results that will measured in these ways" during the requiring process.

A role map is a performance map with authorities. It adds the authority that an incumbent in a role or job has to do things – the decisions they can make about expending resources, assigning work to people, doing or not doing things and so on.

A role map is necessary for effective performance contracting, since it gives the person handling the role or doing the job clear insight on whether or not there is appropriate alignment between what needs to be done and how it will be measured. It clarifies whether or not the individual has be right to make the decisions and to engage the resources needed to do the things that need to the done in the way that they will be measured. It reflects what needs to be done against the organizational (positional) power the person has to do it.

[17] If there are more, it is really helpful to organize them into 3 to 7 groups. The more senior the position, the more likely this need. See Miller, G. A. (1956). "The magical number seven, plus or minus two: Some limits on our capacity for processing information". *Psychological Review* **63** (2): 81–97. (pdf) or access the Wikipedia article on short term memory at http://en.wikipedia.org/wiki/Short-term_memory.

[18] SMARTE performance objectives answer the following questions.

S: What specific, concrete things will the person be expected to produce, achieve or deliver?

M: How will these achievements be measured? What things will the manager involved see and hear that tell the manager that this objective has been achieved? If it is a matter of degree, how will these metrics by used by the manager to evaluate degree of completion or degree of quality?

A: Can the person act to achieve it? Do they have the authority to mobilize the resources – dollars, people and facilities – needed to do the work to produce these specific things in a way that meets the measures?

R: What results, i.e. deliverables will be produced? What do they look like? In what media will they exist? How will other people access them, if that is appropriate?

T: What timeframes are involved? By when is each result (i.e. deliverable) to be finished and available?

3. Janine will review the performance map with Maxwell to make sure that is relevant to the to positions for which they are recruiting. She make notes on any updates or changes that are important, and attaches them to the performance map. That way they will become part of the input for the next recruitment for this, or other similar positions.

Out Reach – Attracting Candidates

4. While this is happening, Janine places a preliminary job advertisement on the two "internet" job boards that Widget uses for engineering type positions. One is a large board like Workopolis or Monster or Career Builder. The second is the job board on the local chapter of the professional engineering society. She also posts it to Widget's internal "refer a person you know" page on the company portal. Widget's staff are rewarded whenever person they refer is offered a permanent full time position. The reward program offers them a choice from a menu of options worth $1000.

5. Janine monitors the resumes that come in. She scans them quickly. Wilhelm, her recruiting coordinator, has eliminated the ones that are clearly a misfit. She sorts the rest into No and Possible groups. If enough come in, the No resumes will not receive any further attention. Janine reads the Possible resumes and cover letters in more depth. Based on this second reading, she will again discard the ones that she thinks not right into No pile. When she has about 10 Possibles, she will meet with Maxwell to review them to make sure that they are pulling the right kind of candidates. If not, she will update the job advertisements based on what they have learned.

Preliminary Telephone / Skype Screening of the Early Possibles

6. Janine instructs Wilhelm, her recruiting coordinator in HR, to contact the top 10 or so candidates and schedule a 15 to 30 minute Skye or telephone interview. She prepares three "What would you do in this situation" short cases to use in these interviews. They come directly from the performance map being used for each recruitment. (If there are large differences between the two positions, the questions will be different for each recruitment.)

7. She modifies Widget's "Preliminary Candidate Ranking Form to reflect any particularities needed for this recruitment. The discipline of completing it after each interview moves the recruiter from "subjective first impressions and feelings

---

E: In which environment must the person act to achieve this? Who are the people involved? Who facilities / materials will be used? What dollars are available to pay for the needed resources?

about the candidates" to disciplined judgments that can be explained in words to other people.

8. Janine conducts the Skype or telephone interviews. She tries to get this done as quickly as possible. She completes the Preliminary Candidate Rating Sheet for each candidate as soon as she finishes each interview.

    Once again, she sorts her results into "Possible" and "No Way" groups. At this stage, given that she is recruiting for two positions, she is trying to get at least 8 Possible candidates who are willing to take the next steps.

9. During these first interviews, Janine knows that she also has two other tasks to perform, especially with the candidates in the Possible group. She must sell Widget and determine if there is enough candidate motivation that the person is likely to take the job if offered. So when she starts her telephone or Skype interviews, she carefully sets aside the last 10 minutes of the interview for what she calls "Wrap Up / Next Steps". When based on the interaction she has had so far in the telephone or Skype interview, she feels intuitively good about a person, she will spend this time selling Widget and the job. When she is not positive about a person, she will cut this time down to polite words which say we will get back to you if … .

10. Janine only wants to spend time on selling "working at Widget" to the better candidates at this stage. She is also aware that she can get too enthusiastic about talking about all the great things that make up Widget and its culture. By putting this task at the end, she is better positioned to make this choice and keep the sell short and focused.

11. Janine must determine if each Possible person who gets through the telephone or Skype interview is motivated by this Widget possibility. One part of that relates to compensation. Janine knows what Widget is prepared to pay for these positions. She must determine the person will come for level of compensation, without engaging in an actual salary negotiation. One way of doing that is find out what the person is currently making. Another is ask about salary expectations.

12. As well, Janine is well aware that the best candidates will motivated by things like career progression possibilities and opportunity to learn more than they are motivated by compensation. This will be especially true if they already have a job. Again, Janine will only to start to explore these issues with the Candidates that she believes are likely to make the final Possible group. She is managing a difficult balance here. She want to motivate and intrigue, without getting into actual negotiation at this point.

Checking with the Hiring Manager

13. Janine meets with Maxwell to review her impressions, the resumes and Preliminary Ranking Sheets for the Possible candidates she has identified to date. At this point, her objective is to make sure that Maxwell is comfortable with the people she is finding. It also keeps him up-to-date on the recruitment's progress. She will go through each of the people who are currently in the Possible group with him. She will ask briefly go through one or two of the No Ways. By doing so, she is making sure that her expanding her sense of the intangibles for which Maxwell is looking in a final candidate.

Detailed Interviews with the Individual Candidates who are Clear Possibles

14. Janine now plans a 1 hour interview outline. She prepares 3 to 5 "What would you do in this situation" short cases that deal with typical interpersonal and group work environments in which Widget's design engineers will encounter. She emails them to Maxwell to give him a chance to comment.

15. Janine recognizes that at least 1/3 of each interview again will be spent on selling / informing the candidates about the job and Widget. She plans to deal with this in the last part of the interview.

16. She has asked each long list candidate to bring some sample of the design work that they have done in the past that is relevant to this position. They have received an email from her recruiting coordinator describing about what Widget is looking for. This email also stress that fact that this material will remain confidential to the Candidate and Janine.. Janine knows that she is not technically equipped to evaluate this work. She is more interested in how each candidate behaves in presenting it to her, and what steps they take to illustrate their abilities. At the same time, she will be curious about what steps the candidate has taken to remove the identity of the firm for which they worked. The ability to do confidential work that is of interest to Widget's competitors is a big part of these jobs. The right candidates will know that this is an issue based on their past job experience, and will take steps to "cloud" this identity.

   Finally, Janine modifies the two template rating sheets that will be used in the rating of candidates throughout this search. The first is "How will do you think this person will perform on-the-job". It deals with the ability of candidates to perform in this job. The second is "How will do think this person will fit into our culture at Widget". It covers the fit of the candidate's personality to Widget's culture. Both ask individuals to make subjective judgments, in the form of predictive ratings, based on their interaction to date, with a candidate.

17. Wilhelm, Janine's recruiting coordinator, arranges face-to-face interviews with the top 8 to 10 still active candidates. Janine tries to get them done as quickly as possible. Since she is recruiting for two positions, she and her recruiting

coordinator have some leeway in this. Once they have 3 strong final candidates for the first position, they can start to deal with the final candidates for the second.

In the meantime, resumes are still coming in. If there is a particularly strong one, Janine will ask her recruiting coordinator to fit in a Skype/telephone interview. Based on this, the candidate may be added to the Possibles list, since experience has shown that there is a good chance that people will drop of this recruitment process based on events in their job search, or at their current organization, if they are employed.

At the end of each interview, Janine completes the two rating sheets. They will form part of the data pool that is eventually used to assess candidates.

Starting to Involve the Hiring Manager and Future Co-workers

18. As she finds the time, Janine works on her briefing notes for "peer – potential co-worker" and hiring manager involvement with the final candidates. She has asked Maxwell to identity these folks for her.

19. She knows that her briefing meeting with these folks will be a crucial meeting. During it, she will educate them about Widget's recruiting process and their part in it. She will explain the two rating forms to them. She will show them an example of how their ratings are summarized in a way that pushes their personal identity into the background. She will explain that the pattern and the spread of the ratings will be most important element in assessing the final candidates. She will stress that these are to be filled out independently, before the individuals talk to one another to share their impressions of the final candidates. These ratings are best done quickly, within an hour working hours of each person's meeting with each final candidate.

She will to explain that there will be two cycles of this process, one for each position for which they are recruiting. She will stress that at this point in the search it will be very important for them to flex to the candidate's schedule, even though it may mean disrupting their own.

Finally, she will give each person a copy of Maxine Bridot's video presentation on the importance of recruiting effectively to Widget. She hopes that knowing that the CEO stresses this will help deal with the inevitable upset that people feel when their work schedules are impacted by recruiting needs.

20. Janine meets with Maxwell again. By now, she has 5 Possibles who seem to be well motivated. She is continuing to search for more as things move forward. Based on Janine's review, Maxwell accepts four of the five. Together they rank them from 1 (most desirable hire) to 4, based on what they know to date. Maxwell thinks that the fifth candidate does not have the right mix of relevant

technical experience. He is clearly not impressed with the fifth candidate. Janine drops this person.

21. Once she and Maxwell are done, they immediately move onto the meeting with the group of co-workers who will participate in the final candidate meetings. Janine briefs them as she has planned. She concludes by introducing them to Whilhem, her recruiting coordinator. Whilem will be sending them all the forms and resumes they need, as well as doing the scheduling of meetings.

Briefing the Short List Candidates to Perform

22. Wilhelm, Janine's recruiting coordinator contacts the three highest ranked Possibles candidates and arranges for them to come in to meet with co-worker/hiring manager group. He sends each of them a set of preparation instructions. At the same time, he sets up a 5 to 10 minute Skype/telephone appointment for each person with Janine, which will happen 1 to 3 days before their meeting with this group. In this meeting, Janine will brief each person on what to expect and how to get ready. She will also use this meeting to just stay in touch with each of these candidates, doing her best to keep their motivation and interest in Widget high.

23. At the same time, Wilhelm make sure that each of the coworkers and managers will be available for these meetings. It has all been made easier by tentatively penciling in several times in the next week when these meetings could happen.

24. Janine continues to search for more Possible candidates. In the meantime, she holds the preparation Skype/telephone briefing meetings with the current possible candidates scheduled by Wilhelm. She tell them:

- Prepare a short briefing (10 minutes or so –use PowerPoint) on presentation on "what I would do in this situation" for 2 scenarios that they have been sent by email. In each case, cover both how they would deal with the technical challenges, and the way they would work with peers and others to get the work done. Identify any risks, and indicate what they will do to cope with them.

- Expect to make this pitch to hiring manager and 3 to 5 future working peers in a face to face meeting.

- Expect to answer their questions afterwards.

- Expect the entire meeting will last 45 to 60 minutes, depending on level of activity during meeting.

Assessing Performance Fit and Cultural Fit

25. Janine facilitates the face-to-face meetings between the Final Possible candidates, the hiring manager and the peer group. She manages the structure and process, but stays out of the discussions, acting as an observer when they are going on.

    When the meeting is over, Wilhelm, her recruiting coordinator, picks up the candidate. Janine stays with the group. She asks them to fill out their rating forms before they leave the room. As well, she invites them to send her emails with their impressions and comments on each candidate. She makes sure that they know that they can do this by phoning her if they prefer.

    As they fill out their forms, Janine once again completes a set of her own. Janine knows that Wilhelm will also fill out the "How will do think this person will fit into our culture at Widget", based the impression that he has of each Final Possible Candidate. He will do this as soon as he has escorted the person out of the building.

26. Wilhelm summarizes rating sheets using codes (M = manager involved, C = coworkers, R = recruiter, S = recruiting coordinator) so that the summary sheets show the rating spreads. Janine reviews them, and meets with Maxwell.

    They jointly decide on the ranking of the top three final candidates. Janine asks Maxwell if he wants to meet the top ranked individuals personally again, or if he is ready to make an offer at this point. Maxwell indicates that since the people ranked 1 and 2 are so close, he would like to meet both if Janine has found no stronger candidates in her on-going interviews. .He thinks that once he has met them, it might make sense to offer jobs to them both, and short circuit the continuing search. Janine accepts this possibility, but indicates that she will continue to do first round Skype / telephone interviews with other possible candidates just in case. Maxwell agrees that this makes sense. They both know that strong candidates are managing their own job search and could very well find another position, eliminating them from taking a job at Widget.

Hiring Manager Interviews

27. Wilhelm sets up the face to face meetings with Maxwell for the top two ranked candidates. Janine follows up with Maxwell by phone after he is done. He tells her that he wants to offer the individual ranked 1, but is less sure about the person ranked 2. He wants to meet the third person who presented to them before he is sure. Janine starts Wilhelm on setting up the meeting needed. In the meantime, she has phone conversations with the two candidates that Maxwell has met.

She has discussed salary expectations before with each of these folks. So she knows that the offer will be in the range expected by the person to whom Maxwell wants to make an offer. She tells him to expect the formal offer by courier first thing in the morning. She talks with the other person and does her best to put the person "on hold". However, she senses disappointment. Janine tells the individual that she understands that he might have to consider other offers in the meantime She is not too concerned, since there are several other strong candidates showing up in her continuing interview process.

28. Janine receives a telephone call that the offer has been accepted by the first ranked candidate. She calls Maxwell and informs him. Wilhelm contacts the person who accepted the job offer to start the on-boarding process.

On-boarding the First New Hire

29. Janine holds the first "on-boarding" briefing session with Maxwell. She talks about with him about who will act as peer "coach / mentor" for the newly hired person during the first four weeks. This will be somehow other than Maxwell. It should be someone who the newly hired individuals sees as a peer.

    She takes Maxell through about "confidential" follow up rating sheets (How I think this person is performing on-the-job" evaluation rating sheet and "How I think this person is fitting into our group" rating sheet). They identify the four people, in addition to Maxwell, will be asked to fill these out. These are folks who are likely to interact with the new hire, and see how the person does in this time period.

    At the same time, Janine informs Maxwell that the new hire will also be asked to complete a: "How I think …. " version of them. The ratings will be completed at the end of week 6 and at week 10 of the 12 week probation period. In the first 6 weeks, Janine will have short check in conversations, each week by phone with the new hire and Maxwell. If there is any sign of troubles, she will take steps to find out more, talking to the new hire's On-boarding coach as well.

Early Performance Evaluation to Catch Any Bad Hires

30. Once the rating sheets are summarized at the end of week 6, Janine will meet with Maxwell first. During her meeting, Maxwell will provide his perceptions about how well the person is doing on the performance metrics that Janine prepared as part of the performance map.

31. Once Janine is clear on all of this data, she will meet with the newly hired person. If things are going well, this meeting will be relatively straight forward. Wilhelm will schedule short check in conversations with Maxwell and the new hire for each of the next three weeks.

32. If things are not going well, Janine will have to provide that feed back to the new hire and develop a "let's make things better" plan with the person. Maxwell must be fully on board with these improvement steps. Janine will have talked these possibilities through with him before meeting with the new hire. Janine will also arrange to meet weekly with the person, after checking in with Maxwell in each of the next three weeks.

33. Wilhelm schedules the collection of the rating sheets at the end of week 10. He summarizes them, gives them to Janine, and sets up the meetings with Maxwell and the new hire.

34. Janine and Maxwell go through Maxwell's perception of the performance of the newly hired person. After this meeting, Janine decides if the probation termination clause needs to be executed. If she decides yes, she informs Maxwell and takes the appropriate steps to bring the person's employment to an end. If not, she will start the process of confirming permanent employment at the end of week 12. At that point, the new hire transfers to Maxwell's authority. Janine will not be actively involved from this point on.

35. During the first weeks of the new hires probation period, Janine and Wilhelm continue to do the things necessary to find a person for the second position. Once that person accepts an offer, they set up and manage a similar on-boarding and progress evaluation process for the second new hire.

Quality of Hire is the Key Hiring Effectiveness Metric

Widget's recruiters are not just interviewers who pass candidates onto hiring managers. They are responsible for managing the entire "early performance" and culture fit assessment. They are accountable for acting on problematic hires, ensuring that they do not become full time employees. If there are problems, through coaching, the newly hired person has a chance to "adapt" to Widget performance environment. If they cannot, they are terminated. To make this easier, Widget's offer of employment describes this process. It also clarifies new hires are rarely asked to leave Widget. If they are, they are given two month's salary to ease the transition. Janine knows that Widget's hiring process weeds out poor candidates early. She also knows that the care taken to on-board the candidate is highly contusive to ensuring that they are enthusiastic and well oriented to their new jobs.

Widget's recruiting process is one example of the "better way". But it is demanding. Widget's recruiters need a number of skills beyond just interviewing.

1. They must facilitate meetings.

2. They must educate hiring managers and co-workers about their roles in the hiring process, on boarding and early performance evaluation process.

3. They must be able to conduct data gathering interviews and translate the results into performance maps, which contain accurate, observable 3 month and 1 year performance metrics.

4. They must be able to sell Widget and the job opportunity to candidates.

5. They must be able to motivate candidates to consider Widget's job offers seriously, concurrently developing and assessing their motivation to come to Widget, especially if they are already currently well employed.

6. They must be able to coach new hires during their first crucial 12 weeks with the company.

7. They must be capable of mediating/ resolving conflict originating in differing perceptions about how a person is doing on-the-job.

They are recruiters with a difference equipped with the skills and the job authority to deal with realities of 21st century hiring, where the demand for skilled, highly motivated people generally exceeds the supply.

Widget's gets three great benefits from their work.

1. First, weak candidates are weeded out early, saving the company a great deal of expense, and Widget's existing staff a great deal of stress.

2. Second, bad hires are avoided. Recruiters who have this "live with the consequences of your recruiting decisions" responsibility tend to be sharper, better recruiters. The basis on which they evaluate candidates shifts from "how do they do in the interview" to "how well will they perform on-the-job". That is where the real payoff from recruiting comes.

3. Finally, the new hires who participate in this process deepen their commitment and loyalty to Widget. They feel that they are "important" to Widget from the first day they arrive at the job. They see people taking steps to help them get comfortable with their new responsibilities. They are exposed to performance metrics early in their time at Widget, understanding how shared performance metrics decrease the political posturing between superior and subordinate, and improve performance focused communication between them.

They feel appreciated from day 1, a feeling that turns into higher levels of performance that lasts long after their 12 week probation period.

Appendix: Two Sample Performance Maps

One: Receptionist

Two: Ruby Agile Software Developer

Performance Map: Receptionist, Willowby Customer Services
(An Example)

Performance Map: Receptionist, Willowby Customer Services			
Objective or Task	**1st 3 months**	**1st Year (after 1st 3 months)**	**Performance Metric**
Learn the duties of the receptionist thru training from the outgoing individual in the post. (by end of 2nd week)	Take over full responsibility for the receptionist role from 9AM to 12PM and 13PM to 17PM when the current receptionist leaves (2 weeks after start of work).		See the metrics below.
Greet all individuals who enter the office and direct / connect them to appropriate people within WCS	Get know all WCS staff and what they do (by end of 30 days) Greet all incoming individuals (store coats etc, drinks etc) (by end of day one) "Park" individuals who come in and do not have a name for the person who they want to see – connect to office manager to sort out (by end of day 1)	Handle all incoming individuals, regardless of their state, including individuals who come in without a name for the person who they want to see – understand their needs and direct them to an appropriate WCS individual	No visitor is directed to the wrong WCS individual, even when visitors are not clear on who they want to see. No one enters the main WCS office without being appropriately "screened" during the times the receptionist is on "duty"

Performance Map: Receptionist, Willowby Customer Services			
Objective or Task	**1ˢᵗ 3 months**	**1ˢᵗ Year (after 1ˢᵗ 3 months)**	**Performance Metric**
Monitor the "info@WCS.com" inbox and handle incoming e-mails appropriately	"Spam" in the inbox is properly discarded (by the end of week one) Valid emails are directed to the appropriate WCS person, including the office manager if it is unclear as to who the email should be directed	All these e-mails are handled either through discard (spam), through forward to the appropriate WCS individual, or through direct reply email. The office manager does not need to get involved unless the e-mail message is directly relevant to the office manager's job.	No info@ e-mail is handled incorrectly. Senders do not complain their e-mails was lost or not responded to. WCS staff do not have to re-direct e-mail messages to other WCS individuals when they are forwarded to them.
Monitor the "general WCS" voice mail box and handle messages left there appropriately	Voice messages that do not require action are discarded (by the end of week one) Valid voice message directed to the appropriate WCS individual, including the office manger if it is unclear as to who the voice message should be directed	All these voice are handled either through discard (no action required) or through forward to the appropriate WCS individual, or through direct reply phone call. The office manager does not need to get involved unless the voice mail message is directly relevant to the office manager's job.	No voice mail message left in the general voice mail box is handled incorrectly. Callers do not call again to complain their e-mails was lost or not responded to. WCS staff do not have to re-direct voice messages to other WCS individuals when they are forwarded to them.

Performance Map: Receptionist, Willowby Customer Services			
Objective or Task	**1st 3 months**	**1st Year** (after 1st 3 months)	**Performance Metric**
			In WCS's periodic customer satisfaction surveys, questions about interaction with the receptionist are answered positively.

Performance Map: Ruby Agile Developer, XYZ Internet Software Services[19]
(An Example)

Performance Map: Ruby Agile Developer XYS Internet Services			
Objective or Task	**1st 3 months**	**1st Year (after 1st 3 months)**	**Performance Metric**
Become capable at using the software development platform used by the team: 1. Software development workstations used by each pair programming team 2. Servers and test tools used to run relevant parts of accumulated test suite against new code 3. Code check in / check out process for running daily application builds 4. Time sheet	Work with your pair programming team member to acquire these capabilities. (1st level of capability by the end Month One, complete capability by the end of Month Two).	Become capable of training/ coaching/ mentoring others on the use of the items in the software development platform.	By the end of month three, no questions about how to use these tools are being directed to other team members. No "mistakes" on your part in the use of these tools impact the ability of the project team to meet their daily, weekly … delivery targets. By the end of the year, a new individual assigned to your programming pair reports that you have taught them the use of these tools in 30 days, as part of your

---

[19] This firm uses a "pairs" programming approach when software development projects create applications that have not been built before. In pairs programming, two people work side by side when developing / writing software code. Although this seems like duplication of work at first, the shared creativity of two minds leads to better software solutions in the long run, especially when there is no history of building similar applications in the firm. Also, having two pairs of eyes involved during the code writing process can significantly decrease the number of "bugs" in the resulting computer code. As a result, projects complete faster, and software code goes into production with significantly fewer bugs. The initial investment in pairs programming can reduce the long term cost of software development, transition into production and future "bug" elimination. At the same time, pair programming requires deeper levels of interpersonal skill on the part of the programmers. See the Wikipedia article on pairs programming for more insight and discussion. http://en.wikipedia.org/wiki/Pair_programming

Performance Map: Ruby Agile Developer XYS Internet Services			
Objective or Task	**1st 3 months**	**1st Year (after 1st 3 months)**	**Performance Metric**
application used to log work times 5. Team / office wiki software used for communication in project team and in the office in general			doing project work.
Participate in a pair programming team, writing Ruby and Ruby on Rails code for the project tasks assigned	The code that you and your partner developer is submitted on time and generally (> 60%) does not derail the daily app build process.	The code that you and your partner developer is submitted on time and generally (> 90%) does not derail the daily app build process.	The reports generated by the various tools in the software development platform. The shared review of daily app build done in the regular team standup status meeting.
Interact with the "user representatives" for the project code development segments" assigned to your programming pair once the code is ready for release to them. Collect their teed back and modify the code that	User reps sign off on the final versions of the app segments / features your programming pair works on.		User reps comment that their feedback is taken into account and leads to appropriate changes in the code for the app segments / features your programming pair

Performance Map: Ruby Agile Developer XYS Internet Services			
Objective or Task	1st 3 months	1st Year (after 1st 3 months)	Performance Metric
has been developed as appropriate.			works on.
Participate in the regularly scheduled project team "stand up status" meetings, and in team problem solving meetings as requested to by the team project manager.	Share responsibility for making "status" updates about your assigned with the other member of your programming pair (by the end of month one).	In addition to making status updates, initiate follow up with other project team members when their status updates indicate a need to coordinate your programming pair's work with theirs. When requested by your project manager, you participate in problem solving meetings with other team members, contributing based on your knowledge and past experience.	Other members of the project team seldom (<10% of the time) ask clarifying questions after your status updates. Other team members comment on positive level of your contribution when asked by your project manager. Some of the solutions developed in the project solving teams you work in are fully or partially the result of your contributions.
Do the personal professional development work assigned, thereby increasing both technical and		You complete the personal development assignments you agree to in discussion with	Your work incorporate some of the new technical approaches that you have learned

Performance Map: Ruby Agile Developer XYS Internet Services			
Objective or Task	**1st 3 months**	**1st Year (after 1st 3 months)**	**Performance Metric**
interpersonal skills		your project manager and your organization's HR training lead.	in day to day work. You take on more complicated technical assignments that these new skills allow you to handle by the end of the year. You get generally positive results (> 80% of the individuals rated you positively on > 80% of the elements) on the anonymous "working with others" survey conducted by your organization's HR folks in the 2nd to last month of each year.

Section Three

"Achieving Enterprise Results through Personal Delivery"

"Increasing Individual Ability through Personal Professional Development"

Employee / Leader Work Book

Note:
This is the generic version of a handbook developed for the leaders and professional staff in an organization that changed its performance management process from:

Backward looking Performance Appraisal

To Forward Looking Performance Contracting

combined with formal
Performance Evaluation.

Part One: Introduction

1.0 Your Enterprise's Approach

Most enterprises today are committed to managing their staff performance through personal performance agreements and concrete measure-based personal performance evaluation. The objective behind these two processes is to help you focus on what you need to do your job successfully. At the same time, the dialogue between you and the person who is your designated Manager allows each of you to align with your enterprise's overall performance goals. When everyone in your organization is aligned in this way, the organization will achieve its goals. That means better results for all of us, results that are reflected in our salaries and bonuses[20].

Your organization is also committed to helping its staff members grow their on-the-job competencies and skills. We call your manager your "Manager" to emphasize this and remind each of you that you need to be constantly aware of the inter-locking nature of your responsibilities around performance agreement, performance evaluation, and professional development.

The ultimate responsibility for developing yourself rests with you. Your Manager can motivate you, guide you, and provide you with important feedback. When appropriate, your Manager can help you get access to relevant training programs and educational resources. However, in the final analysis, the only person who can increase your abilities is you. **ONLY YOU CAN TAKE RESPONSIBILITY FOR DEVELOPING YOURSELF.** No one else can do this.

Performance Contracting (PPA/PPE) and Professional Development (PPD) are separate processes with distinct goals. Each impacts the other. But they are distinct processes, with different steps and timings. All of this will become clearer in the detailed descriptions of each process, which follow later in this work book.

Performance Contracting is the organization's process for ensuring that its employees know what they have to deliver, and for evaluating the extent to which they do so. It consists of two interlocked processes: Personal Performance Agreement (PPA) and Personal Performance Evaluation (PPE).

Personal Professional Development (PPD) is your process for expanding your competencies and skills, so that you can do your current job better, and prepare yourself for future positions with more scope and responsibility.

---

[20] Copies of sample Personal Performance Agreements and Personal Performance Evaluation Policies are provided in the Appendix at the back of this work book.

From this point on, Personal Performance Agreement will be abbreviated as PPA: Personal Performance Evaluation will be abbreviated as PPE and Personal Professional Development will be abbreviated as PPD.

2.0 Accountabilities (Who is responsible for what?)

The following table clarifies who is normally accountable for what during PPA and PPE activities.

Process	Manager	Employee
Personal Performance Agreement (PPA)	Initiate the dialogue with each employee, which establishes a PPA for the coming performance period. (Do this for each employee in turn.)	Participate in the dialogue.
	Ensure that a signed PPA exists before the performance period starts.	Understand the PPA well enough to commit to producing these deliverables: that is what signing it means. You are committing yourself to delivering these results in the coming period.
	Make sure to send a signed copy of the PPA (either in paper or in an electronic copy with electronic signatures) to the appropriate HR person.	Receive a copy and keep it in your personal files.
Personal Performance Evaluation (PPE)	Initiate the dialogue by asking the employee to self-rate achievement on each of the items in the PPA for this period.	Rate your achievements on each item, using the results reported for its associated KPI, Measure, or Evidence of Accomplishment.
	Rate the employee's	

Process	Manager	Employee
	achievement on each item in the PPA for this period. Base your ratings on the reported KPIs, the Measures, or the Evidence of Accomplishment associated with each item.	
	Schedule and lead the meeting in which the two ratings are compared. Resolve any differences, if you can. Make notes about any that you cannot resolve.	Participate in the meeting.
	Finalize the PPA form based on the meeting and ask the employee to sign it.	Sign it if you agree with it. Add any reservations that you have if you do not agree.
	Make sure to send a signed copy of the PPE (either in paper or in an electronic copy with electronic signatures) to the appropriate HR person.	Receive a copy and keep it in your personal files.
Personal Professional Development	Initiate the dialogue by asking the employee to fill out the ability self-rating sheet with respect to his / her current position.	Complete the ability self evaluation with respect to your current job Think about your competency strengths and weaknesses,

Process	Manager	Employee
	Complete the ability rating sheet for this employee with respect to his / her current position.	generating ideas on how to improve your abilities.
	Schedule and lead the meeting in which the employee's self-evaluation is compared to your ratings (The Manager's). Move the dialogue forward by focusing on self-development activities that are appropriate for this employee and that the employee is motivated to complete.	Summarize the results of the meeting in a self-development action plan for yourself for the next 12 months (follow the suggested format in this work book). Sign the action plan, and send copies to your Manager, and to the appropriate person in Human Resources.

3.0 Timelines (When to do …)

The Personal Performance Agreement (PPA) process cascades down the organization from the Strategic Directions set by the Your Enterprise's Executive group and your Board in the late fall of each calendar year for the next year[21].

In the table which follows, a normal calendar year is assumed. The dates used are suggestive. You organization may have somewhat different ones.

As well, a simple organizational structure is assumed. The CEO reports to the Board. Executive Vice Presidents (EVPs) report to the CEO. Vice-Presidents (VPs), and perhaps the occasional Director, report to EVPs. Most Directors, and perhaps the occasional Manager, report to VPs. Managers report to Directors.

The term "Manager" is used generically. It covers any reporting relationship in which one person – the Employee – reports to another – the Manager, regardless of where the relationship falls in the organization's organizational hierarchy.

---

[21] For some organizations, this process may be aligned with fiscal year, if the fiscal year is not the same as the calendar year.

Personal Performance Agreement (PPA), Personal Performance Evaluation (PPE), and Personal Professional Development (PPD) dialogue timings are all related to the scope of the employee's job.

The following table provides the suggested timings. The intent behind this table is simple: provide a suggested framework that your organization can modify when it implements or updates its own PPA/PPE/PPD processes.

Who	Job Scope / Normal Work Cycle	PPA Completion	PPE Completion	PPD Dialogue
CEO and EVPs (the CEO's direct reports)	CEO – all of the enterprise. EVPs – the major operational / functional units of the organization. (E.g. operations, manufacturing, accounting / finance, sales / marketing, human resources, information technology) Calendar / Fiscal Year	December 15th of each calendar year	December 1st of the following calendar year (aligned with end of PPA)	January 30th
VPs (report to EVPs)	Part of each of the major operational / functional units Calendar / Fiscal Year	December 15th of each calendar year	December 1st of the following calendar year (aligned with end of PPA)	January 30th
Operational / Functional Unit Directors (report to VPs)	Part of each VP's part of a major operational / functional unit Calendar / Fiscal	January 15th of each calendar year	January 1st of the following calendar year (aligned with end of PPA)	February 15th

Who	Job Scope / Normal Work Cycle	PPA Completion	PPE Completion	PPD Dialogue
	Year			
Working Group Managers (report to Directors)	Part of each Director's sub-unit of a VP's part of a major operational / functional unit Calendar / Fiscal Year	January 15th of each calendar year	January 1st of the following calendar year (aligned with end of PPA)	February 15th
Working Level Employees (report to Managers)	Individual worker Calendar / Fiscal Year	January 30th of each calendar yea	January 1st of the following calendar year (aligned with end of PPA)	February 15th
Project Staff (report to Project Managers)	Project life time	Within a week of the designated project or program start, updated as often as needed during the life of the project	Within a week of the formal completion / close of the project	As appropriate

Part Two: Personal Performance Agreements

1.0 KPIs, Measures, and Evidence of Accomplishment

Performance evaluation that is not based on objective evidence is extremely frustrating to staff. Countless employee satisfaction surveys have validated this. Working level staffs express extreme frustration with performance evaluation they consider "gamey". They disengage when they believe that managers play "favorites", basing their performance evaluation on personal subjective like and dislike, rather than negotiated and agreed to performance metrics. As a result, individuals are not motivated to make the best contribution that they can make to achieve your organization's collective results

Performance evaluation (or performance appraisal as it is called in some organizations) needs to be grounded on concrete facts in order to avoid the "subjective, personal, and political". By making sure that staff members know how they will be measured or evaluated on each of the objectives in their Personal Performance Agreement, all or most of the negative reactions to performance appraisal can be avoided. Individuals may still experience negative emotions during this type of performance contracting. However, when a performance contracting process is based on concrete metrics, these feelings occur when individuals are held accountable for their non-performance. That is appropriate and necessary.

The key is clarifying the KPIs (or Key Performance Indicators), Measures, or Evidence of Accomplishment associated with each item in each person's Personal Performance Agreement. This will be done at the beginning of the performance period. That way, each employee knows:

- what they are expected to do in order to make a valued contribution to your organization,

- how they will be evaluated on their performance at the end of their performance period,

- and most importantly, how **to take stock of their performance during the performance period**, so that they can take steps to improve their delivery, or ask for help with difficulties from their designated Manager.

1.1 What is a KPI?

A good example of a KPI is "Revenue Dollar per Employee Wage Dollar". It shows how much revenue each employee in your organization produces. It is a "unit of output produced per unit of input used to produce the output" ratio. Put simply, it is an output/input ratio. The output is dollars of revenue earned; the input is "dollars of labor cost of the employees". Specifically, it relates the revenue produced in a time period to wages paid to employees who produce that revenue in the same time period. For a non-profit organization, the number of "services delivered" might replace revenue. These kinds of ratios are relatively easy to create. They are limited only by the underlying quality and structure of the information that the organization keeps.

By following the trend of such KPI's, you can see if your organization is getting more or less productive over time.

This example illustrates the **four defining** characteristics of a KPI.

4. It is **a ratio**, which results from dividing one number by another number.

   These numbers can come from any of the information systems (accounting, operating, marketing …) that you use to manage and to work in your organization.

5. The **time periods** for the two numbers must match in a way that makes business sense.

   For example, the Revenue per Employee number can be calculated for a year, a month, a quarter, a week, or any other useful time period. The input number must cover the same time period.

   Because automated business applications have limitations on how they collect and store information, KPIs are often calculated for months, quarters, and years. Occasionally, it is also possible to calculate them for days and weeks.

6. The organizational scope of the two numbers must match in a way that makes business sense.

   For example, the Revenue per Employee number can be calculated for an entire organization, a business unit, a geographical unit, or subsets of any of these. The input number must match the output number's scope.

   Because automated business applications have limitations on how they collect and store information, KPIs are often calculated for the entire organization, and its major sub-divisions. It is also possible to calculate down to the department, work unit level. In fact, defining KPIs for individuals, teams, and work groups is an important part of the PPA process.

7. KPIs are **most useful** when they presented as trends over time, rather than as single point-in-time values.

We want to look at the trend in the Revenue per Employee KPI, rather than its value at any one point in time. If the trend is going up, then we know that the revenue being produced per employee is getting better.

Note:
Because we want to look at trends, we can use mathematical tools like the trend line tool in EXCEL (or other software programs) to draw a trend line over a series of values for a KPI like Revenue per Employee. Excel uses excellent statistical tools to do this. We don't need to worry too much about the tools themselves, so long as we remember they are just a tool for doing a job. We could do much the same thing by plotting the KPI on a graph manually, and then using a ruler and pencil to fit a trend line by hand. Excel and other software simply make this much easier to do.

1.2 How are KPIs used?

When you measure the results achieved on a performance objective in a PPA with a KPI, you are saying that the trend in the KPI will improve over the time period covered by the KPI.

For example, the CEO's PPA could include an item like this.

Objective	How will the results achieved be measured?
Improve your enterprise's use of its main talent asses – employees – in both the short term and the long term.	KPI – Revenue Per Employee: the monthly trend improves over the course of 2010 and the 2010 trend in Revenue Per Employee is better when compared to the 2009 and 2008 trends

Notice some important things about this objective and KPI, which apply to all performance objectives and their KPIs.

The CEO is not told HOW to do this. That is up to the person in the job.

It does show how the CEO's results in this area will be measured. The exact use of the KPI is stated. There is little room for confusion.

If the CEO agrees to this performance objective, the CEO is also agreeing to how its achievement (or lack of achievement) will be measured.

The result is a very focused item in the CEO's performance agreement. It is now up the CEO to take action to achieve this. For the CEO, this might be setting strategic priorities and communicating them to other employees in the organization. It might mean creating more specific performance objectives in the performance agreements of the employees who work directly for the CEO. It is up to the CEO to decide how this objective can best be achieved.

This is why it is called a PERSONAL PERFORMANCE AGREEMENT. The dialogue between the Manager and the Employee (in this case, between the CEO and the organization's Board) is about WHAT needs to be done, and WHAT measurements will be used to evaluate results. The PPA itself does not contain the HOWs.

You will want to take the same approach in both the performance agreement dialogues you have with your Manager and those you have with your staff, if you are a Manager.

You want to keep the HOWs out of Performance agreements.

That does not mean that you do not talk about HOW. **Of course you do** - all through the year in your coaching sessions and in your problem-solving work with your co-workers. By talking about HOW in these settings, and keeping them out of PPAs, you focus on what is important in PPAs:

Objectives – what must be achieved,

and

Measurement of Results Achieved On Those Agreed on Objectives - the measurement techniques used to evaluate the achievement of these results.

1.3 When does it make sense to link KPIs to performance objectives?

KPIs are very powerful performance achievement evaluation tools. Choose them when the following conditions are in place.

1. Producing the KPIs, and plotting their updated values on a graph for each time period (days, weeks or at minimum months) is straight forward to do. The results must be available and reported to all involved in the performance objective in a very TIMELY FASHION, so that everyone has the chance to act on negative trends and reverse them[22].

---

[22] Business Analysts in Finance, or in an Operations Statistics group, may be able to help with the analysis and reporting to produce timely KPI reports

2. The employee has **the authority to do things** that can positively impact the trend in the KPI.

    For example, the CEO has the authority to ask employees to do things that can positively impact revenue per bus. A recruitment professional in Human Resources does not. This KPI makes sense for the CEO, but not the recruitment professional.

    Setting performance objectives, and associated KPIs, for an individual, when the individual does not have the personal authority to get the things done needed to positively impact the achievement of that KPI is a WASTE OF TIME. It leaves individuals feeling like they have been "gamed" by their Manager. It can undermine the whole performance contracting process.

1.4 Cascading Down Levels of KPI

Too many organizations set KPIs only at the organizational level. They then tie every bonus's to these KPIs, in the belief that somehow people will figure out how to align their personal performance with achieving these broad reaching KPIs. In fact, one of the prime tasks of management is to break down such organizational wide KPIs into more specific ones relevant to each level of the organization. Managers are responsible for structuring and coordinating the way in which work is done in the organization. That is the PRIME task of management.

Because of this, one of the best KPIs for manager is the EXISTENCE OF KPIs that derive from the ones they receive from their Manager and cascade down into ones for the people who report to them.

Sometimes, doing this is simple. For example, a CEO could take the Revenue per Employee KPI, and break into down into Revenue per Employee in each business unit. Often the only limitation keeping this kind of break down from cascading down to the individual level are limitations built into the information processing applications the organization has in place.

At other times, Managers must demonstrate real creativity in coming up with KPIs that are relevant to individuals. They must get beyond the limitations in information applications, and creatively set up KPIs that really help an employee understand how their contribution will be measured. Doing so is part of the challenge, and the fun, of being a Manager.

The KPI must clearly support your organization's current Year's Strategic Priorities and long-term business directions. Asking employees to deliver on performance objectives that are NOT aligned with the overall strategy, rarely makes good business sense.

1.5 What is a Measure?

A measure is simpler than a KPI. It is a number or an item. Its distinguishing characteristic is that is used in a YES or NO way. The measure is either achieved or not. The item either exists or not. There is no in-between.

A good example of a measure is a monthly report. Let's say an employee has a performance objective to produce a report for the previous month by the 10th working day of the following month. Let's look at this example in more detail.

Objective	How will the results achieved be measured?
Produce and distribute the monthly "Parts Used Maintenance Facilities" by the 10th working day of the following month.	The report is distributed on time by email using the IT Network to all Maintenance Facility Leads at their local facilities and all Maintenance Managers in the organization's head office each month.

This means that the person with this performance objective has to fail to deliver in one month in order to NOT meet this measure. **Measures are binary: – yes or no, achieved or not, exists or not.**

There may be extenuating circumstances for not achieving a measure. The person's Manager may agree that the explanation for not achieving the measure is reasonable. The Manager may talk about this during coaching sessions. HOWEVER, none of this eliminates the fact that the measure **has not been achieved**.

The strength of a measure is that it makes WHAT must be accomplished crystal clear. The limitation inherent in measures is that there is no room for partial success.

1.6 How and when are measures used in a PPA?

As a Manager, choose measures (as opposed to KPIs or Evidence of Accomplishment) for performance objectives that MUST be achieved.

As an employee, only agree to measures that you believe you can achieve.

Of course, it is always possible to structure the measure to create some degree of flexibility. The measure above could have been written as follows.

The report is distributed on time by email using the IT Network to all Maintenance Facility Leads at their local facilities and all Maintenance Management staff at Head Office at least 9 out of the 12 months. In the months when it is not on time, there is a clear reason for the delay that is beyond the control of the individual producing the

report. In each case that this happens, the individual informs all of the recipients of the report of the reason for this delay by the 8th working day of the month.

This is still a binary measure. The person either achieves it or not. Now there are a number of specific conditions that create more business room for the person who commits to achieving it.

Remember that you have this degree of flexibility as you create and agree to measures in PPAs.

1.7   What is Evidence of Accomplishment?

Sometimes the only way to know if something has been achieved is if a number of people can observe a new pattern of behavior or a new way of doing things. When the achievement of a performance objective is measured in this way, we are looking for evidence of accomplishment. The key is that more than one person can see the evidence. Its achievement is verified by reports from multiple sources.

Objective	How will the results achieved be measured?
Decrease the level of complaints and dissatisfaction of customers with the service being provided at the Jonesville Location (123 Jones Street, Jonesville).	Most or all of the following occur and are reported: • Conversations between the Customer Service Manager in this location and other Managers in the organization change from negative to positive in tone starting in February of this year. • Talking to the Jonesville service delivery staff about how customers are feeling about service delivery changes from a mostly negative experience, in which they blame others as being responsible for their service delivery problems, to a mostly positive experience, in which they are positive about their ability to service customers.

There are several kinds of evidence listed in the Measurement column. Although each is relatively clear in and of itself, collecting evidence that they have occurred is not as simple as looking at numbers or the line on a graph.

In this case, this Manager will have to take the time to talk to a number of people to collect details on the evidence. Judgment will have to be applied in interpreting what they each say. A decision will have to be made if the perceptions of these individuals make up a pattern that shows if the Evidence of Accomplishment has been achieved.

The key to Evidence of Accomplishment is always that more than one person perceives it and is willing to report on it. Accomplishment requires agreement across a number of sources.

1.8 How and when is Evidence of Accomplishment used in a PPA?

KPIs and Measures are always the preferred way of measuring whether or not results have been achieved. However, it is not always possible to use them for all performance objectives. This is especially true when the performance objective contains subjective elements (e.g. level of customer satisfaction, change in tone from negative to positive). However, these are real results with real business value.

Evidence of Accomplishment is a useful way of measuring such results.

Coaching is another area which is often best measured by evidence. See the following example taken from the PPA of a person responsible for overseeing a number of local service delivery managers.

Objective	How will the results achieved be measured?
Coach the local Service Delivery Managers as they work to achieve this year's reduction in average hours per service call objective while increasing the customer satisfaction per service call.	Evidence of Accomplishment: Local Service Delivery Managers who have the highest "hours per service call" and the highest number of Customer Complaint calls change their behaviors in the following ways. • They interact with the Centralized Service Technical Dispatch call center to get immediate and up to date information on the service calls their service staff have performed each month. • They make a point to meet with

Objective	How will the results achieved be measured?
	or to call each service delivery person at least once every two weeks, getting them to talk about the problems they are facing in servicing customers. • They use the weekly Customer Complaint Call summary issued by the centralized Customer Service call center to focus on difficulties with service calls in their areas, and take steps to eliminate repetitive problems. Conversations with the local Service Delivery managers indicate that they have receive coaching throughout the year that has helped them accomplish these things.

2.0 The Personal Performance Agreement Checklist

The following table lists the activities that are involved in preparing for, discussing and completing a Personal Performance agreement. Use it as a checklist for yourself in your role either as a Manager or as an employee.

The activities covered are:

1. Pre-planning

2. PPA Dialogue / Negotiation

3. Commitment to Act, To Deliver

4. Filing

5. Coaching

6. Updating the PPA

Activity	Manager	Employee
Pre-planning	Prepare for a PPA conversation by listing the items that the employee is expected to deliver in the coming performance period. Use past year's PPAs, job descriptions, and PPA templates provided by Human Resources during your planning. Group your list into three to seven performance objectives. Remember that most people, especially at the "doing" level in the organization, will need to focus on a few key objectives, NOT on long lists of activities and things to do.	Prepare for your PPA the conversation by listing the things that you are accountable to deliver. Use your last PPA, or your job description, and your on-going coaching discussions with your Manager as a starting place. Organize your work into three to seven key performance objectives. Note: Most people are most comfortable if they have about three to five performance objectives on which to concentrate.
	Identify appropriate KPIs (Key Performance Indicators), Measures, and Evidence of Accomplishment observables so that each item in the "expected to deliver" list has one associated with it. Make sure that you have at least one for every performance objective. Make sure that the information needed for the KPIs and Measures exist, and can be easily and regularly reported to the employee and yourself in a TIMELY fashion.	

Activity	Manager	Employee
	Remember that feedback which arrives too late to act on is de-motivating, while no feedback at all is frustrating.	
	Organize the "items to be delivered" and their associated KPIs, measures, or observable evidence into your organization's PPA format (see a sample later in this work book). If it is more than two pages, and the employee does not report to the CEO or an EVP or a VP, it is probably too long. Re-organize the performance objectives. Shorten the list by moving to a higher level of objective. Make sure that you are NOT including HOWs in the PPA.	
PPA Dialogue / Negotiation	Pass the draft PPA to the employee before the performance period begins.	Review the draft PPA and prepare for the PPA conversation with your Manager. • Compare the draft to your own list. • See if anything is missing in the draft PPA. Plan to talk about it. Review each of the KPIs, Measures, and Evidence of Accomplishments. • Do you understand

Activity	Manager	Employee
		it? • Do you see how it relates to its performance objective? If you have any concerns, plan to talk about them.
	Schedule and lead the meeting. • Cover each performance objective. Talk about how each item in the Measurement column relates to each item in the Objective column. • Listen to any concerns or ideas. Consider changing either the objective m or the measurement item related to it. • If the employee talks about HOWs, listen, respond positively, and take note. This is good material for you to use in coaching sessions. However, do not incorporate HOWs into the PPA. Point out that the PPA is about objectives and measurements, not about how to achieve the objectives. • Mark up your copy of the draft PPA with the agreed-upon changes. End the meeting by stating that you	Participate actively in the meeting. Raise your concerns. Ask the questions that you need to understand each performance objective and the measurement items related to it. Remember that, because of this meeting, you will be asked to commit to achieving these performance objectives in the coming period. So this is an important meeting. You are contracting on: • What you will be expected to do in the next months, and • What measurements will be used to evaluate the extent to which you achieve these results?

Activity	Manager	Employee
	will make them and send the final PPA to the employee to review once more.	
Commitment to Act, To Deliver	Update the draft PPA, making the changes that came out of the meeting. Print two copies of the final version, one for the employee, and one for you one for filing with HR. Note: At some point, this whole process may be part of an automated business application. At that point, electronic copies and electronic signatures will replace the paper. However, paper copies of the PPA are very important at this point. They act as tentative contracts. Psychologically, they exist outside of our minds. They are disassociated embodiments of the contract which is about to be made. Reading and signing paper copies of contracts has great RITUALIZED meaning in most Western cultures.	
	Send or give a copy of the final PPA to the employee. Ask for any final suggestions for changes. If the employee has more suggestions, either make them, or clearly communicate why they are	Review the final PPA. It should be complete, especially if you have communicated any concerns you might have had about the draft during the meeting. If you do have any final concerns or changes, talk to

Activity	Manager	Employee
	not appropriate. This is best done in another face-to-face meeting.	your Manager about them.
	Schedule a short meeting to sign the final PPA. Bring three copies, one for the employee, one for you, and one for filing with HR. Ask the employee to sign all three copies. Then sign them yourself. Signing a PPA is an important act of organizational ritual. It symbolizes the fact that: <ul><li>The employee is committing to delivering the performance objectives.</li></ul><ul><li>You are committing to using these measurements to evaluate this person's performance.</li></ul><ul><li>You are committing to coaching this employee - to help them as they need and ask for help on the HOWs needed to deliver these results.</li></ul>	Participate in the meeting. Sign all three copies if you are: <ul><li>Committed to delivering these results,</li><li>Expecting to be evaluated at the end of the performance period based on these measurements.</li></ul> <ul><li>Expecting your Manager to ensure that you get regular feedback on these measurements in your coaching sessions, and coaching on the HOWs that you need to achieve these results.</li></ul>
Filing	Give one signed copy to the employee, keep one yourself, and send one to the appropriate person in Human Resources. Note: This last copy is there to make sure that a copy exists in case events lead to a change in circumstances. For example, you may move to another position during the performance period, and not be able to transmit your	Keep your copy. Refer to it during your coaching sessions.

Activity	Manager	Employee
	copy of the PPA to the person who replaces you. The copy at Human Resources will fill in this gap.	
Coaching	Meet regularly to provide feedback and coaching advice. Use the KPI and Measures reports as part of these sessions. Take steps to collect facts on the Evidence of Accomplishment all the way through the performance period. Report your ongoing results to the employee. Talk about the HOWs – especially if the KPIs, Measures. and Evidence indicate that this employee is not going to deliver on his / her performance objectives. Help them improve their performance.	Participate in your regular coaching sessions. • Review your KPI and Measures reporting. Interpret the trends. Decide on what you need to do to either improve things, or keep them going the way they are. • Talk about your insights with your Manager. • Ask for help if the Measurements indicate that you are having performance problems. Take action now; don't wait until the end of the performance period.
Updating the PPA	Remember that a PPA is contract that was made given a set of business conditions. A contract is valid only as long as the people who originally signed it agree that it is valid. If business conditions change and you want to change the PPA, raise the possibility with the employee and see if there is room to re-negotiate all or parts.	Remember that a PPA is a contract that was made given a set of business conditions. A contract is valid only as long as the people who originally signed it agree that it is valid. If you see significant business change that impacts your ability to meet your performance objectives, raise the issue

Activity	Manager	Employee
	If there is, take care to go through all the steps needed to produce a new one. Sign it and ensure that it explicitly states that it is replacing an existing one.	with your Manager. Talk about the potential of re-negotiating parts or all of the PPA.

3.0 Some Samples of PPAs

The following pages contain some samples of PPAs. Use them as a guide. Follow their format in your own PPAs.

Personal Performance Agreement for Rod Davidson, Time Frame: Jan 2010 to Dec 2010
Regional Area Manager, Metro Service Region, Wilnet School Bus Services

	Objective	How will the results achieved be measured?
Day to Day	Oversee the improvement of the profitability of the delivery of contracted school bus services in the Metro Service Region while customer satisfaction and employee engagement stays stable or improves.	**The following results are achieved at each of the five operating sites in the Metro Service Region.**
		KPI: Operating Revenue/Driver Wage for each operating location (CSC) in the Region improves with respect to last school year and over the course of this school year
	Oversee the local General Managers running each of the five operating sites within the Metro service region. Ensure that they accomplish their operating improvements within the framework of Wilnet's policy and automated standardized work flows.	**Measure:** Operating Expense Lines are Under Budget Line Amounts over the course of the Fiscal Year at each site
		Measure: Operating Profit line in each site's P&Ls is positive and improving over the course of the fiscal year.
	Override the GM's day to day management ONLY to correct negative performance issues, or when the size and scope of an issues exceeds the work scope of the geographic boundaries of the Metro service region, or when it has negative impact on the company as a whole.	**Measure:** Operations Audits indicate that all local operating Practices align with Wilnet Policy, and that local operating practices align with Wilnet standard work flows and processes (manual and automated).
		Measure: Preventable Street Accident Frequency and Total Injury Frequency decline over time.
	Oversee the local General Managers as they work with Driver Recruiting / Training, Corporate Human Resources, Corporate Finance, Bus Maintenance Services, Corporate Facilities Management, Corporate Purchasing and Customer Relations Management to steward the staff and the assets used to deliver school business service to clients.	**Measure:** Each site's Employment Engagement scores on the Employee Satisfaction survey are at last year's level or better.
		Measure: Customer Satisfaction scores on the Customer Satisfaction survey are at last year's level or better.
Coaching	Conduct regular coaching sessions with local General Managers to help them improve their site and personal performance	**Measure:** At least 20 1 hour coaching sessions are held with local operating leaders each month.
As required over the course of the year	Direct the General Managers as they collaborate with Customer Relationship Management to re-negotiate customer contracts or win new business during 2010.	**Evidence:** The Regional Area Manager and the Site General Managers are involved in contract renewal and new business initiatives in the Region during 2010.
	Support Business Maintenance Services in their work to deliver maintenance unit cost improvement over the course of 2010	**Evidence:** Local operating staff utilizes maintenance procedures, and work to ensure that "driver avoidable" maintenance work is eliminated or minimized.

Agreed: (RAM) _____ on _____ (dd) _____ (mm) _____ (yy)
                  Rod Davidson

Agreed: (Leader-Manager) _____ on _____ (dd) _____ (mm) _____ (yy)
                  Kathy McClusin – Vice-President, School Bus Operations

Personal Performance Agreement for Wilamena Hernandoz: Time Frame: Jan 2010 to Dec 2010
General Manager, Operating Site One, Metro Service Region, Wiinet School Bus Services

	Objective	How will the results achieved be measured?
Day to Day	Deliver "On Time, Every Timer" service to customers in an accident free way that increases the Operating Site One's profitability without having a negative impact on customer satisfaction or employee engagement: • Run Routes • Handle Parent/Customer Calls not handled by Corporate Customer Call Center • Do local work need to Steward Drivers and other local staff (other than Maintenance staff), under guidance of Driver Recruitment / Training and Corporate Human Resources Handle local paper work not handled by Corporate staff, using standardized work flows and automated business applications • Invoicing (AR) • Route records • Customer contract records • Driver records • Staff records • Facility records • Bill records (AP)	**KPI:** Operating Revenue/Driver Wage for the Operating Site One improves with respect to last school year and over the course of this school year **Measure:** Operating Expense Lines for Operating Site One are Under Budget Line Amounts over the course of the Fiscal Year **Measure:** Operations Audits indicate that all local operating practices at the site align with Wiinet policy, and that local operating practices align with Wiinet standard work flows and processes (manual and automated). **Measure:** Preventable Street Accident Frequency and Total Injury Frequency decline over time. **Measure:** Employment Engagement scores for Operating Site One on the Employee Satisfaction survey are at last year's level or better. **Measure:** Customer Satisfaction scores for Operating Site One's customers on the annual Customer Satisfaction survey are at last year's level or better.
As required over the course of the year	Collaborate with Customer Relationship Management to renew contracts with existing customers or win new customers Collaborate with Bus Maintenance Services staff to improve the operations of the maintenance facilities	**Evidence:** The General Manager is involved in customer contract renewal and new business initiatives for Operating Site One's customers during 2010. **Evidence:** Local operating staff follow maintenance procedures, and work to ensure that "driver avoidable" maintenance work is eliminated or minimized.

Agreed: (GM) _____ on _____ (dd) _____ (mm) _____ (yy)
Wilamena Hernadoz

Agreed: (Coach-Leader) _____ on _____ (dd) _____ (mm) _____ (yy)
Rod Davidson, Region Area Manager

Part Three: Personal Performance Evaluation

1.0 Performance Evaluation Summary Rating

When based on the KP/s, Measures, and Evidence of Accomplishments included in PPAs, Performance Evaluation is a concrete, fact-based process. Both the employee and the Manager can approach the discussion with confidence. They both know what the evaluation will be based on. They both have been tracking performance progress over time, and discussing it during their regular coaching sessions.

During performance evaluation, the Manager must summarize the employee's performance for the past performance period in a summary rating. Each of the points on a five-point scale on the scale is described below.

5 Performance Dramatically Exceeded Performance Measures

This employee has delivered at a level that has exceeded all Measures in the employee's PPA – perhaps even doubling the delivery expected on the majority or most of them.

4 Performance Exceeded Some Performance Measures

This employee has delivered at a level that has met all of the KPIs, Measures and Evidence of Accomplishments at the expected level, and has exceeded delivery on at least half of them, particularly on those of the most importance or weight.

3 Performance Achieved Most or All Performance Measures

This employee has delivered at a level that meets most or all of the KPIs and Measures.

If the employee has not achieved on one or two of the Measures, it is clear that events beyond the employee's control have kept him / her from doing so. The employee **has communicated** with you during your coaching sessions about this potential lack of delivery. The individual **has clearly taken actions** intended to correct the situation.

2   Execution Does Not Meet 50% of Performance Measures

This employee has delivered at a level that has not delivered on 50% of the Measures. There are no clear reasons for this other than the individual's own performance. This pattern has become clear over the course of the year during your coaching sessions. The employee initiated dialogue with you about these issues, and was proactive about taking steps to reverse this situation. There is clear evidence that things are on an improving trend. This pattern will not be repeated.

1   Execution Is Severely Below Performance Measures

This employee has delivered at a level that has not most or all of the Performance Measures. There are no clear reasons for this other than the individual's own performance. The individual **has not communicated** with others about this potential lack of delivery, and has not taken **actions** to correct the situation.

During your coaching sessions during the performance period, the employee has been available to change their performance to reverse this pattern. The employee might have attempted but shown little or no sign of success.

You cannot leave this employee this in position, but must take remedial action.

In most cases, the "Performance Achieved Most or All Performance Measures" rating will apply.

2.0 The Performance Evaluation Checklist

The following table lists the activities that are involved in preparing for, discussing, and completing a Personal Performance Evaluation. Use it as a checklist for yourself in your role either as a Manager or as an employee.

The activities covered are:

1. Pre-planning: Performance Items

2. Pre-planning: Summary Measure

3. Dialogue

4. Performance Evaluation Form Completion and Signing

5. Filing

Activity	Manager	Employee
Pre-planning: Performance Items	Prepare for a PPE conversation by reviewing the employee's PPA, and any notes that you have made as a result of your coaching sessions throughout the performance period. Summarize your evaluation of the employee's performance **on each item** in the PPA during the performance period, using the 1 to 5 scale described several pages back. Base your evaluation on the associated KPI or Measure or Evidence of Accomplishment associated with each item. Prepare to provide the employee with details on how you reached this conclusion for each item. Note: In the case of Evidence of Accomplishment, talk with the people you need to gather the evidence you need. Summarize it carefully. Prepare to share the information that you have in a way that presents the GENERAL PATTERNS of what people have said, NOT "he said or she said" specifics. If you have been discussing performance progress based on KPIs, Measures or Evidence regularly during your coaching sessions with the employee, this will be a straight forward summary of these dialogues.	Prepare for your PPE conversation looking at the items on your PPA and evaluating your accomplishment on each one, based on the KPI or Measure or Evidence of Accomplishment associated with each one. Note: If you have been doing this regularly during your coaching sessions with your Manager, this will be a straight forward summary of these dialogues.

Activity	Manager	Employee
Pre-planning: Summary Rating	Based on your item-level preparation, rate the employee's overall performance during this period on the summary rating. Remember that it is YOUR RESPONSIBILITY as this person's MANAGER to make this judgment at this time. It is important that you LOOK AT THE PERSON'S CONTRIBUTION FROM YOUR ORGANIZATION'S POINT OF VIEW WHEN YOU MAKE THIS JUDGMENT. Record your summary evaluation on a draft copy of the evaluation form (format provided later in this work book). Forward the draft to the employee, Prepare for the meeting. See Section 3: The Likely Performance Evaluation Scenarios above –for guidance on this step. Note: "On Summary Ratings" Some Managers calculate their summary ratings as a simple mathematical average of the individual item level ratings. This assumes that each item is of equal importance to your organization, since each item receives the same weight in this procedure. Others pay attention to the more important performance items, and provide more weight to these. If you are mathematically inclined, you can actually assign weights to	

Activity	Manager	Employee
	each item, and then calculate a weighted average. One easy way of doing this is to take 100 points and distribute them across the item, giving more to the more important ones, and less to the less important ones. (Using a 100 1-dollar bills or coins is a very powerful way of doing this, which helps you to think and to feel through all of the issues in doing so.) **Of course, if you think that this process is appropriate, you SHOULD DO THE WEIGHTING as part of the original process of agreeing on the PPA in the first place. That way there are no surprises for the employee at the end of the performance period.**	
Dialogue	Meet with the employee. Discuss each performance item, resolving any differences you have on your perceptions of the results achieved based on the associated KPI, Measure, or Evidence of Accomplishment. Discuss the summary rating, resolving any differences that you might have. Remember that it was YOUR RESPONSIBILITY as this person's MANAGER to make this judgment at the end of the performance Period. Your role is to evaluate this person's contribution to your organization	Meet with your Manager. Discuss each performance item, resolving any differences you have on your perceptions of the results achieved on the associated KPI, Measure, or Evidence of Accomplishment. **Listen** to your Manager's presentation of your Summary Rating, and the reasons for it. Remember that it is your MANAGER'S RESPONSIBILITY to make this judgment ABOUT

Activity	Manager	Employee
	when you make this rating, not "get along" with the employee if he or she disagrees with your judgment.	YOUR PERFORMANCE at this time. Your Manager will be looking at your contribution during this past performance period from your organization's point of view. Your Manager will be acting as an ENTERPRISE Leader for the short period when making this rating, not as your COACHING Manager. If the two of you have been engaged in regular, open coaching sessions, in which you have realistically discussed your performance delivery and achievement based on your KPIs, Measures .and Evidence of Accomplishment, this summary rating will not be a surprise to you.
Form Completion and Signing	Complete the final copy of the Personal Performance Evaluation, and forward it to the employee for signing and comment. Ensure you make three copies. Give one to the employee, keep one, and send one to the appropriate person in Human Resources.	When you receive the final copy of the Personal Performance Evaluation Form, sign it in the appropriate place, and add your comments. Return it to your Manager. Receive a copy of the signed from your Manager

3.0 Likely Performance Evaluation Scenarios

The fact that both the Manager and the Employee independently prepare their version of the summary rating creates the following possible "agreement / disagreement" scenarios. The appropriate way of handling each situation is described below.

Possibility	Manager Handling	Follow up required
General Agreement Manager and Employee generally agree on the extent to which each KPI, Measure, or Evidence has been achieved. Employee accepts Manager's summary rating.	Complete the performance evaluation form. Have the employee sign it. File a signed copy with Human Resources, keep a copy for yourself, and give one to the employee.	Move onto Personal Performance Agreement for the coming performance period. It is best is done in a separate meeting, several days later.
Some agreement on details, but disagreement on the summary rating Manager and Employee agree on the extent to which many of the KPIs, Measures, or Evidences have been achieved, but are substantially in disagreement on one or two major ones. As a result, the employee does not accept the Manager's summary rating.	Complete the performance appraisal form. Indicate the areas of agreement and disagreement. Ask the employee to sign the portion of the form indicating disagreement with the summary rating. Point out that doing so requires that the employee write a note explaining why there is disagreement. File a signed copy with Human Resources, keep a copy for yourself, and give one to the employee.	Move onto the next period's Personal Performance Agreement. Pay particular attention to sharpening the concrete nature of the KPIs, Measures, and Evidence of Accomplishment, Over the course of the period, during your coaching sessions, cover these in depth, attempting to ensure that any difference of perception is dealt with long before the formal performance evaluation.
Serious disagreement on the details. No Acceptance of the Summary Rating Manager and Employee do not agree on their perceptions of the extent to which most the KPIs,	Complete the performance appraisal form. Indicate the areas of agreement and disagreement. Ask the employee to sign the portion of the form indicating disagreement	**Manager**: approach your own Manager and discuss what you can do to turn this situation around before you begin the Performance Agreement process for the next period. If necessary, approach the

Possibility	Manager Handling	Follow up required
Measures, and Evidence of Accomplishments have been achieved. Employee does not accept Manager's summary rating. **This is a serious problem**. The Personal Performance Agreement and regular coaching sessions in which performance progress is reviewed are intended to avoid this. In most cases, getting to the final performance evaluation with this level of disagreement indicates that these have failed.	with the summary rating. Point out that doing so requires that the employee write a note explaining why there is disagreement. File a signed copy with Human Resources, keep a copy for yourself, and give one to the employee.	appropriate person in Human Resources for advice as well. **Employee**: Take steps to improve the specific the concrete nature of the items in your next period's Personal Performance Agreement. Make sure that you understand what each item means, and that you are very clear about how each KPI, Measure, and Evidence of Accomplishment will be used to evaluate your performance. Prepare rigorously for your coaching sessions. Make notes about the extent to which you are achieving your KPIs, Measures, and Evidence throughout the performance period, not just at the end of it.

4.0 The Personal Performance Evaluation Form

Because PPEs are tied to an individual's PPA for this performance time, the Manager will prepare the first draft of the form as part of Pre-Planning activity. A template for doing so follows.

WilNet School Business Services

Personal Performance Evaluation for Wilemana Herandoz, General Manager, Operating Site One, Metro Service Region

Time Frame: Jan 2010 to Dec 2010 **Completed by:** Rod Davison, Region Area Manager

Section One: Delivery on PPA Objectives

(List Objectives Below)		Performance Achieved				
		1-Did not Achieve	2 Achieved	3 Exceeded	4- Dramatically Exceeded	Notes/ Comments
Refer to PPA	1.					
	Manager's Notes					
	2.					
	Manager's Notes					
	3.					
	Manager's Notes					
	4.					
	Manager's Notes					
	5.					
	Manager's Notes					
	6.					
	Manager's Notes					
	7.					
	Manager's Notes					

WilNet School Business Services
Personal Performance Evaluation for   Wilemana Herandoz, General Manager, Operating Site One, Metro Service Region
Time Frame: Jan 2010 to Dec 2010   Completed by: Rod Davison, Region Area Manager

Section 2: Overall Evaluation

1 Severely Below Performance Measures	2 Did Not Meet 50% of Performance Measures	3 Achieved Performance Measures	4 Delivery has Exceeded on Some of Performance Measures	5 Delivery Dramatically Exceeded Performance Measures
This person has delivered at a level that did not meet a number of the KPIs and Measures..	This person has delivered at a level has less than 50% of the performance measures. However, the person has initiated corrective action, and it is clear that this pattern will not be repeated.	This person has delivered at a level has met most, if not all of the KPIs, Measures and Evidence of Accomplishment. The individual acted to fix any problems before the end of the period	This person has delivered at a level has met all of the KPIs, Measures and Evidence of Accomplishment at the expected level, and has exceeded delivery on at least half of them, particularly on those o	This person has delivered at a level that dramatically exceeds all KPIs, Measures and Evidence of Accomplishments.

Section 3: Signatures and General Comments

Leader-Manager Signature	Dated (dd/mm/yyyy)	Comments and Notes
Employee (I agree with my overall rating.)	Dated (dd/mm/yyyy)	Comments and Notes

To the Employee: If you DISAGREE with your Overall Performance Rating, please sign below and NOT ABOVE.
If you do so, you must attach a SIGNED and DATED Note to this form which describes the reasons for your disagreement.

Part Four: Personal Professional Development

1.0 What is Personal Professional Development (PPD)?

Personal Performance Agreement and Personal Performance Evaluation are your organization's tools for focusing employees on the contributions they are expected to make. Skill Development is **your tool to improve your ability to make contributions**. It is your tool to increase your capability, to expand your skills and to equip yourself to take on roles with more job scope and responsibility.

Skill development processes are competency based. You manage your skill development by identifying competency gaps. These gaps describe the difference between what you can do now, and what you might need to be able to do to improve your performance. It works as follows.

You use a competency dictionary to assess your current perceptions of the skills you have.

You ask your Manager to assess the extent to which you are demonstrating the same set of skills in your current role.

By comparing these two perceptions, you identify competency gaps. You then dialogue with your Manager on action plans to address these gaps.

Of course, your Manager is not the only person you can talk to about developing your competencies. You can talk to your co-workers, educators at Community Colleges / Universities, and HR professionals. The Internet is also a rich source of ideas about competency development.

Skill development is your responsibility. You are free to do any one of a number of things that will help you achieve your skill development goals. Although your organization will support you in various ways, you **must demonstrate the initiative** in this area. Your career future is something that you must actively manage. Personal skill development is the key to making this happen.

2.0 What are competencies and how do you use them?

In the past 20 years, there has been extensive work on developing competency dictionaries for organizations. Essentially, these are long lists of competency definitions. All of this work, in many organizations, has uncovered three important things.

There are two kinds of competencies: **technical** and **social / interpersonal**.

The contents of the competency dictionary are less important than the way they are used to identify skill gaps. (This is true as long as the list of competencies is reasonably robust. Use competency lists that are similar to the ones used by most organizations in an industry, and you will not go wrong).

Technical competencies are the crucial core of performance in a job. They are job specific, base level skills without which people cannot do their job.

However, the difference between the average performer and the best performer in a role **is defined by their level of social competencies**, provided both have a good level of technical skill.

Your Manager (or a Human Resources professional) can help you understand the essential technical competencies for your role.

Note:
For example, "driving in line with the local state traffic and safety regulations" is a technical skill for drivers. Using Microsoft Office to prepare documents, spreadsheets, and presentations is a technical skill required of office workers.

Technical competencies are very job specific. The most important ones are usually listed in job ads that you might come across. Your organization generally covers technical competencies under the label "Job Knowledge". **Discuss what this means for your job** with your Manager in order to break "Job Knowledge" down into more specific technical competencies that you can use to develop your skills.

3.0 Your organization's social / interpersonal competencies

Many organizations have developed a list of social / interpersonal competencies that contribute to performance on-the-job. One such list follows below. All of the items on the list have to do with personal or interpersonal factors that allow you to interact more effectively with others on-the-job. (This is what the word "social" in a work context means.)

Competency
Communication Listening, speaking, and writing skills; frequency and impact of communication skills such as persuasion and negotiation.
Customer Satisfaction Degree and quality of involvement with customers (external and internal), including courtesy, respect, and resolution of disputes.
Teamwork and Cooperation Willingness to help others accomplish team objectives and tasks.

Competency

Planning and Organizing
Extent and effectiveness in achieving established goals and developing logical organizational steps to improve processes or programs.

Accountability
Extent of responsibility and authority to establish plans and measures of performance, to commit and direct resources, assess and respond to business and operating conditions, and provide value to the customer (external and internal).

Problem Solving
Degree of complexity, novelty and frequency that issues and problems must be addressed and resolved on an individual job or organizational basis using procedures and analysis to facilitate problem solving.

Leadership and Team Building
Ability to guide and direct; taking the initiative; being creative; providing vision and motivation; future oriented; ability to strategize; model corporate values.

Judgment and Decision Making
Process of reaching a position after the consideration or exploration of various alternatives. Requires the use of own expertise or that of others. Takes ownership for goals achieved or not achieved.

Employee Development
Ability to identify employee development needs by assessing current and future competency levels, and in support with the needs of the organization, effectively develops employee skills and abilities.

Financial Responsibility
Extent to which the incumbent controls, directs, or influences the organization's financial resources and assures the efficient management of them.

Employee Relations
Provides appropriate feedback; effectively communicates with employees; fosters trust; consistently motivates and recognizes employees.

Attendance
Extent to which the incumbent has consistent attendance.

Your Manager, or a member of the Human Resources department, can help you access the list used in your organization. You will probably find that it differs in detail, but not in overall scope.

4.0 What are the steps in Personal Skill Development?

Developing your personal skills is best done by following a step-by-step process.

The steps in the process are:

1. Pre-planning

2. Planning Your Feedback

3. Dialogue with Your Manager

4. Approaching the People You are Asking for Feedback

5. Doing Your Gap Assessment

6. Planning Your Development

7. Acting

8. Repeating the Cycle

Details on each step follow in the table below. Look at each step in succession. Begin by skimming all of the steps. Your purpose on this first pass is to get a sense of the whole. Spend more time on understanding the detail of each step as you complete it in turn.

4.1 Step One: Pre-planning

Activity	Employee	Manager
Focusing	Decide on what you want to focus in this cycle of personal skill development: technical skills or social/ interpersonal competencies. Note: Generally, it makes sense to focus on Technical Competencies first and Social	

Activity	Employee	Manager
	/ Interpersonal Competencies second. There is no hard and fast rule about this. However, remember that, if you focus on too much, you decrease the chances that you can focus your "change energy". You are better off focusing on a few skills, and improving them, than trying to deal with many competencies at once, and spreading yourself too thin.	
For Technical Competencies / Skills	Identify five to seven core technical competencies that are essential to doing your job. You can start by doing one or more of the following. : • Talking to your co-workers or friends who do this type of work. • Talking to an educator in a Community College or University. • Doing some research on the Internet. Schedule a meeting with your Coach Leader. Share what you have found out through your pre-planning. Ask her or him what are the most important technical competences to success in your current job.	If you asked to have this dialogue with one of the people in your area of responsibility, tell that person what you think the core technical competencies for their current position are. Note: Remember that a competency is behavior that other people can see. They judge that a person has a competency by what the person does and the results the person produces. For example, a driver who is competent to drive a bus of a certain size can drive the bus under all road and traffic conditions. (That is what a driving test is intended to determine). Similarly, a person who can perform a trend analysis for a KPI produces the spreadsheets and the graphs for that KPI with

Activity	Employee	Manager
	Summarize your meeting by making a working list of these technical competencies. Note: This is useful work. Share your results with your co-workers or with the folks in Human Resources.	the trend lines plotted on them. That is how others know that the person has this ability. If you are unsure about the core technical competencies for this role, you can do one of the following: • Talk to your own Manager. • Talk to your co-workers and peers and get their insights. • Talk to an individual in Human Resources to see if they can guide you to material that helps.
For Social / Interpersonal Competencies	Get a copy of your organization's Social /Personal Competencies (see the sample list a page or two earlier, or the form in the next step.) Make sure that you understand what each one means. If you have any questions about any of items, do one of the following. • Discuss it with your Manager. • Talk to your co-workers to see if they have any insights. • Talk to an educator at a Community College	If you are unsure of how to answer the "what does this mean" questions from a person in your area of responsibility about the list of social / interpersonal competencies given a few pages ago, do one of the following: • Talk to your own Manager about it. • Talk to your co-workers and peers about it and get their insights. • Talk to an individual in Human Resources (for all roles others than driver / monitor) or a person in Driver Care Manager to see if they can guide you

Activity	Employee	Manager
	or at a University. • Do some research on the Internet. If none of this helps, contact Human Resources for guidance on how to find out more. Once again, you are better to focus on a few at a time in your development action planning. However, getting feedback on your current level on all of them is a good place to start. Once you have it, then you can select the ones around which you want to plan your personal development.	to material that helps. The list provides a definition of each one. However, for many people, clarity comes when they can relate specific examples from their job context to these definitions. Perhaps the most useful response to such questions will be to provide examples of how the competency can contribute to the questioner's effectiveness in her or his current role.

4.2 Planning Your Feedback

Activity	Employee	Manager
Deciding on Who to Ask	The best way to get feedback on the extent to which you exhibit competencies on-the-job is to use a 360° approach. This means that you ask people "all around" you to give you **structured feedback** on how they see you **behave on-the-job**. "All around" you means: From above, - that is your Manager. From beside you, that is peers that you interact with on a regular basis on the job – your coworkers or customers	

Activity	Employee	Manager
	or outside people with whom you interact. From below – that is people for whom you are the designated Manager. Note: People often appreciate being approached to provide this kind of feedback, especially if you tell them that it is part of your personal skill development program. You can also tell them that you will do the same for them. Sometimes, people feel more comfortable giving you "honest" feedback if **they can do so anonymously.** One simple way to do this is to give them the feedback form in a blank envelope. Then they can just leave the completed form inside the blank envelope on your desk some time when you are not at it. Of course, your Manager will not be able to do this, since the form will ask each person to identify his or her perspective with respect to you. That is, they will have to indicate if they are; Your Manager, A co-worker peer or customer or other outside person, or a person for whom you are	

Activity	Employee	Manager
	the Manager. Note: Providing feedback is one of the responsibilities of being a Manager, so this should not be a surprise to individuals in this role. Decide on who should be in your feedback group for this personal development cycle. The options are as follows. • Just your Manager. • Some of your co-worker-peers. You will need at least three but no more than five, if you choose to include this group. • Some of the folks for whom you are the designated Manager. You will need at least three but no more than five, if you choose to include this group. Remember, the closer to 360°, the more effective the feedback will be. However, you do not need include representatives of each group every time you do this. Any feedback is better than no feedback. So choose whom you will ask to be part of your feedback group based on the practical realities of what you are trying to do and	

Activity	Employee	Manager
	your current situation. Prepare the feedback forms that you will need. Adapt the examples which follow.	

For Technical Skills / Competencies

Adapt the forms on the following pages for your own use.

Personal Skill Development
Technical Skills / Competency Feedback

Instructions:

1. You have been requested to provide feedback on the way in which you see demonstrate the following competencies / skills in your on-the-job interaction. _____

   Please base your responses on how you see this person behave when the two of you work together.

2. Please make sure that you fill out the **date** and **Your Role** section on this page (below) before you begin.

3. If you have any questions about the meaning of the any of the skills / competencies, contact the person who asked you to fill out the form.

4. When you are through, put the completed form into a blank envelope and place it on the desk of the person who asked you to do this.

5. Please provide this feedback quickly. It will not take you long to do.
   Getting it back to the person is important as part of their Personal Skill Development program.

Thank You for your participation.

Date Completed (dd/mm/yyyy)	You are this person's Coach-Leader	Peer (You work together as peers)	Your Coach Leader
	Your role and perspective on this person. That is, you are this person's (place x in right box)		This person is

135

Personal Skill Development
Technical Skills / Competency Feedback

Technical Skill / Competency	Rating				
	Not Skilled: Does not demonstrate the skill at all on-the-job. Unskilled / Unaware	**Is Aware:** Talks about the concepts, but shows little or no ability to apply the skill on-the-job to produce results. "Knows that"	**Has Some Ability:** Uses the skill but needs prompting, feedback and coaching from others in most on-the-job situations. Beginning of "Know How"	**Is Practiced:** Uses the skill independently, deciding when and how to use it to get things done in the normal flow of day to day work. Accomplished "Know How"	**Is an Expert:** Applies this competency under all circumstances, including the most difficult ones. Can coach, guide and develop others in the use of this ability. Master and Teacher
1.					
2.					
3.					
4.					
5.					
6.					
7.					

For Social Competencies

Adapt the forms on the following pages for your own use.

Replace the competencies listed if your organization has its own set of social and interpersonal skills.
Contact your HR department to find out.

Personal Skill Development
Social / Interpersonal Competency Feedback

Instructions:

1. You have been requested to provide feedback on the way in which you see

   _____ (name of person)

   demonstrate the following competencies / skills in your on-the-job interaction.

   Please base your responses on how you see this person behave when the two of you work together.

2. Please make sure that you fill out the **date** and **Your Role** section on this page (below) before you begin.

3. If you have any questions about the meaning of the any of the skills / competencies, contact the person who asked you to fill out the form.

4. When you are through, put the completed form into a blank envelope and place it on the desk of the person who asked you to do this.

5. Please provide this feedback quickly. It will not take you long to do.
   Getting it back to the person is important as part of their Personal Skill Development program.

Thank You for your participation.

Date Completed (dd/mm/yyyy)	Your role and perspective on this person. That is, you are this person's (place x in right box)	
	You are this person's Leader-Manager	
	Peer (You work together as peers)	
	This person is Your Leader-Manager	

Personal Skill Development
Social / Interpersonal Competency Feedback

Social Interpersonal Skill / Competency	Rating: **Not Skilled:** Does not demonstrate the skill at all on-the-job. **Unskilled / Unaware**	**Is Aware:** Talks about the concepts, but shows little or no ability to apply the skill on-the-job to produce results. **"Knows that"**	**Has Some Ability:** Uses the skill but needs prompting, feedback and coaching from others in most on-the-job situations. **Beginning of "Know How"**	**Is Practiced:** Uses the skill independently, deciding when and how to use it to get things done in the normal flow of day to day work. **Accomplished "Know How"**	**Is an Expert:** Applies this competency under all circumstances, including the most difficult ones. Can coach, guide and develop others in the use of this ability. **Master and Teacher**
Communication Listening, speaking, and writing skills; frequency and impact of communication skills such as persuasion and negotiation.					
Customer Satisfaction Degree and quality of involvement with customers (external and internal), including courtesy, respect, and resolution of disputes.					
Teamwork and Cooperation Willingness to help others accomplish team objectives and tasks.					
Planning and Organizing Extent and effectiveness in achieving established goals and developing logical organizational steps to improve processes or programs.					
Accountability Extent of responsibility and authority to establish plans and measures of performance, to commit and direct resources, assess and respond to business and operating conditions, and provide value to the customer (external and internal).					

Page 2 of 4

Personal Skill Development
Social / Interpersonal Competency Feedback

Social Interpersonal Skill / Competency	Not Skilled: Does not demonstrate the skill at all on-the-job.	Is Aware: Talks about the concepts, but shows little or no ability to apply the skill on-the-job to produce results.	Has Some Ability: Uses the skill but needs prompting, feedback and coaching from others in most on-the-job situations.	Is Practiced: Uses the skill independently, deciding when and how to use it to get things done in the normal flow of day to day work.	Is an Expert: Applies this competency under all circumstances, including the most difficult ones. Can coach, guide and develop others in the use of this ability.
	Unskilled / Unaware	"Knows that"	Beginning of "Know How"	Accomplished "Know How"	Master and Teacher
Problem Solving Degree of complexity, novelty and frequency that issues and problems must be addressed and resolved on an individual job or organizational basis using procedures and analysis to facilitate problem solving.					
Leadership and Team Building Ability to guide and direct; taking the initiative; being creative; providing vision and motivation; future oriented; ability to strategize; model corporate values.					
Judgment and Decision Making Process of reaching a position after the consideration or exploration of various alternatives. Requires the use of own expertise or that of others. Takes ownership for goals achieved or not achieved.					
Employee Development Ability to identify employee development needs by assessing current and future competency levels, and in support with the needs of the organization, effectively develops employee skills and abilities.					
Financial Responsibility Extent to which the incumbent controls, directs, or influences the organization's financial resources and assures the efficient management of them.					

Rating

Personal Skill Development
Social / Interpersonal Competency Feedback

Social Interpersonal Skill / Competency	Not Skilled: Does not demonstrate the skill at all on-the-job.	Is Aware: Talks about the concepts, but shows needs prompting, little or no ability to apply the skill on-the-job to produce results.	Rating Has Some Ability: Uses the skill but needs prompting, feedback and coaching from others in most on-the-job situations.	Is Practiced: Uses the skill independently, deciding when and how to use it to get things done in the normal flow of day to day work.	Is an Expert: Applies this competency under all circumstances, including the most difficult ones. Can coach, guide and develop others in the use of this ability.
	Unskilled / Unaware	"Knows that"	Beginning of "Know How"	Accomplished "Know How"	Master and Teacher
Employee Relations Provides appropriate feedback; effectively communicates with employees; fosters trust; consistently motivates and recognizes employees.					
Attendance Extent to which the incumbent has consistent attendance.					

Please provide any general comments or observations that will help this person do their person development planning.

1	
2	
3	

Thank you for your participation.

4.3 Dialogue with Your Coach Leader

Activity	Employee	Manager
Discuss your feedback plans with your Manager	Schedule a meeting with your Manager. Talk to her or him about what you want to do. Be clear on: • What you want to focus on this cycle: Technical or Social Interpersonal Competencies. • Talk through your list of people that you plan to ask for feedback. Share why you have included each person in each group. • Ask your Manager to complete the feedback form.	Self-initiated personal development is highly likely to lead to increased competence on-the-job. Be encouraging and supportive with a person who approaches you to talk about his / her desire for competency feedback. Act as a sounding board. Your coaching objective here is to help the person focus on what he or she can realistically do in this period. Review the choice of individuals the person intends to ask to give them feedback. If you have concerns about any of these individuals, raise the issue in a constructive fashion. Talk about how important it is to choose people with whom the employee interacts on a day-to-day basis. Help the employee choose people who are likely to be objective in their feedback. Do not object to any individual if the employee really wants to include them. Instead, if you have concerns, suggest adding one or two more people who are more likely to have the right degree of involvement and are likely to be objective in their feedback. More is always better than less in feedback.

4.4 Approaching The People You are Asking For Feedback

Activity	Employee	Manager
Finalizing Who	When all is said and done, some feedback is better than no feedback. Be practical. Pick people who you know are likely to respond. Make this a useful exercise rather than a perfect one. You can always do it again at some point in the future. A few short steps might get you where you want to be more successfully than one big one.	
Asking Them to Participate	Approach each person. Tell them that you are working on your personal skill development action plan. • Ask them if they will provide you with feedback on your on-the-job demonstration of skills using a form that you have for them. • Tell them that you are asking other people as well, not just them. • Assure them that their feedback can be confidential or anonymous using the blank envelope technique, if that is what they prefer. If they agree, give them a	

Activity	Employee	Manager
	copy of the form that you have prepared. Make sure that it is in a blank envelope. Demonstrating your willingness for the exercise to be anonymous is very important to convincing some people to participate.	

4.5 Doing Your Gap Assessment

Activity	Employee	Manager
Collating the Data	When you get all your feedback forms back, get ready to tally the results on a blank copy of the feedback form. (Print it out – you will want to do this on a paper copy.) Start with your self-evaluation. For each competency, place a clear "**S**" in the rating box which captures your self-assessment of your skill level. Move onto your Manager feedback form. For each competency, place a clear "**L**" in the rating box which captures your Manager's feedback on the skill level you are currently demonstrating. Work your way through each of the feedback forms returned to you by your co-worker /peers. For each competency, place a clear "**P**" in the rating box which captures your co-worker /	

Activity	Employee	Manager
	peer's feedback on the skill level you are currently demonstrating. If more than one person in this group has returned a feedback form, you will have multiple Ps for each competency. In the same way, work your way through each of the feedback forms returned to you by individuals for whom you are the designated Manager. For each competency, place a clear "I" in the rating box which captures each person's feedback on the skill level you are currently demonstrating. If more than one person in this group has returned a feedback form to you, you will have multiple I's for each competency.	
Asking "What does this feedback mean?"	When you are through, you will have a single copy of the feedback form that compares your self-assessment with the feedback that you have received. Spend some time thinking about it. Go through it one competency at a time. Use the following questions as a guide to your thinking. **Make notes on the form that summarize your conclusions and impressions.** The questions to keep in	

Activity	Employee	Manager
	mind…	

Is there a gap between your self-assessment and the observations of others? Does this mean that your impression of your skill level is different from the competency they see you demonstrating in your on-the-job behavior?

Is there a difference between your Manager's perception of the skill level you are demonstrating on-the-job and your self-assessment? If there is, what do you thinks it means? How will you get ready to discuss this with your Manager?

Do your co-worker / peers have a different perception:

- From your self-assessment,

- From your Manager's observation,

- From the observations of the people for whom you are the Manager?

Could it be that your behavior is different with each group? Or is it different with different individuals?

The best way to sort this out is to look at the spread of the P's and the I's. If it is tight (that is, the P's or the I's are

Activity	Employee	Manager
	close together, or all in one rating box), then you are probably behaving in a consistent way with the members of each group. If it is spread out (that is, the P's or the I's are spread out over most or all of the rating boxes), then you are probably behaving differently with each person. In either case, what do you think it means for your on-the-job delivery of results? Consider discussing your impressions with either your Manager or a co-worker that you think has a good perspective on your on-the-job performance. A second insight will always help.	

4.6 Developing your Development Action Plan

Activity	Employee	Manager
Focusing on a few things	Developing your personal skills means changing existing behaviors, or adding new ones. It means unlearning existing habits, learning new ones and practicing them enough so that they become smart habits – things that you can do without conscious though. So it makes sense to focus on just one or two skill areas at time. When you review the results of the gap assessment, pick one or two skills to improve.	If the person approaches you to discuss what they might do to increase their on-the-job skills, remember the following proven facts about adult learning as you coach them. Adults learn best they have an immediate chance to apply the new skills they are learning on real problems and in real situations on-the-job. <ul><li>Learning is a skill that needs to be learned in its own right. If this person</li></ul>

Activity	Employee	Manager
	Discuss them with your Manager. Pick competencies which fit the following criteria: • Improving your skills in this area will improve your delivery on-the-job. • Learning new skills can be done: ◦ through reading books, self learning guides, self-paced e-learning CDs / courses, or research work on the Internet, ◦ using existing your organization's learning resources (talk to Human Resources about this option), ◦ through a coaching / mentoring / learning on-the-job relationship with another person in your organization who can help you develop these skills, ◦ through attendance at a professional development course you can attend, ◦ or through a course at a Community College / University that you can take.	does not have a strong history of past personal self-development, encourage them to start with relatively simple skills, so that they have a chance to successfully learn how to learn. • People stay most motivated to continuously learn if they are recognized for their new abilities. Create opportunities for the person to apply their new skills. Then recognize them publicly for their increased ability and productivity. • Mentoring / coaching relationships are very rewarding for most individuals. They recognize that they are skilled in the area in which they are asked to coach / mentor. Look for opportunities to connect this person with others who can act as a mentors and skill coach to this person. It will be rewarding for both people in the relationship.

Activity	Employee	Manager
	° Note: Some useful research activities. Browse Amazon.com on the Internet and see if there are good learning resources available to you at a reasonable price. Talk to folks at your local Community College / University about what they might be offering in this area. Talk to a co-worker who is clearly demonstrating these skills on-the-job, and ask them how they acquired their abilities.	
Recording Progress	Once you decide on what to do, treat it as a project that needs formal planning and tracking. Use the planning form below to do this. Share it in your coaching sessions with your Manager, so that she or he stays aware of what you are doing.	Encourage and motivate, encourage and recognize. When and if appropriate, help the person access YOUR ENTERPRISE learning resources or get YOUR ENTERPRISE support (e.g. dollars for courses or paid time off work) for personal development activities once a clear development action plan has been developed.

A Sample PPD Goal Setting Form

Personal Skill Development
Goal Establishment and Progress Recording
(Share this with your Coach Leader)

Employee Name: _____

Goal (Example)	Action Steps	Achievement Criteria	Accomplished On: dd/mm/yyyy
Become proficient using Excel to organize financial and operational data into KPIs. Plot the trend results using Excel Line Trend features.	Find an on-line tutorial or book which shows how to use Excel data management, trend line analysis, and plotting features • Arrange access to the computer databases, which contain the relevant information, so it can be extracted and put into Excel. • ... ... •	Completed successfully Access privileges granted by the managers responsible for the relevant databases.	31.1.2010 4.2.2010
Goal #1	**Action Steps**	**Achievement Criteria**	**Accomplished On: dd/mm/yyyy**
Goal #2	**Action Steps**	**Achievement Criteria**	**Accomplished On: dd/mm/yyyy**

Long Live Performance Contracting

Goal (Example)	Action Steps	Achievement Criteria	Accomplished On: dd/mm/yyyy

Comments by Manager (Name:_____)

4.7 Acting

Activity	Employee	Manager
Just Do It	Just Do It	Encourage and support it

4.8 Repeating the Cycle

Personal skill development never stops. Business is always changing. Technology is always evolving. New roles have to be filled.

Once you start on this process, you will likely never stop. Repeat the cycles as often as you want. Sometimes you will start at the beginning (Step One: Pre-planning). Sometimes you will pick a new skill area to focus on (Step Six: Developing Your Development Action Plan). Enjoy the life-long learning journey in which you will always participate.

Appendixes

Appendix One: Sample Personal Performance Agreement Policy

PERSONAL PERFORMANCE AGREEMENT POLICY

Purpose:

To govern the process by which SAMPLE CO. Leaders establish personal Performance Agreements for all SAMPLE CO. individuals.

Note:
Personal Performance Agreement is abbreviated PPA.

Individuals who are contractors to SAMPLE CO. should have performance clauses that are similar in nature to the contents of a PPA included in their engagement and performance.

Principles:

1. Performance Agreement Means Agreeing on Measures

Performance evaluation must be based on concrete measures and KPI's (key performance indicators – expressed in numbers) to be effective. All SAMPLE CO. Personal Performance Agreements (PPA's) are grounded in concrete measures and KPI's. Without them, it is not a PPA.

2. PPA's and Calendar Dates

A PPA is for a specific individual for a specific period. SAMPLE CO. has several "natural" calendar cycles. PPA time periods need to consider these.

- The **operating year runs** from September to August. A number of the significant operating points in it are tied to events in the operating year (semester start, major holidays – e.g. Thanksgiving, Christmas, Spring Break etc, and summer). Individuals who work at the local service locations are most exposed to this cycle. Trends in operating and financial KPIs for this group of staff are often most meaningful on a month-by-month, current operating year to past operating year basis.

- The **fiscal** year – which in SAMPLE CO.'s case is aligned with the calendar year – January to December. SAMPLE CO. Leaders and staff in Head Office experience much of their work structured to meet calendar dates – month end, quarter end, year-end. Trends for this group of staff are often most meaningful on a month by month, current fiscal year to past fiscal year basis

- **Project or program** cycle – which have a start and target date, often referred to as sunrise and sunset days. KPIs and other performance measures are often most meaningful on a "comparison to targeted" milestone date basis.

Generally, PPAs that reflect the operating year are most appropriate for local operating staff.

PPAs that reflect the fiscal year are most appropriate for SAMPLE CO. management and Head Office staff.

Project based PPAs are most appropriate for individuals who work primarily on projects (e.g. IT professionals and individuals assigned to projects).

Variations on these PPA calendar principles require consultation with senior staff in Human Resources.

3. **PPA's are Commitments to Act**

Each person at SAMPLE CO. has a designated coach. Generally, a person's coach is their manager. At times, another individual may be asked to take on this role. Human Resources and the person's Manager must concur with this arrangement.

Most of the time, a person's coach provides feedback and advice which is intended to help the individual reach their best level of performance. However, at the beginning and at the end of each performance period coaches, if they are also a person's manager move out of the coaching role. At the beginning of each performance period, they set performance expectations and clarify how performance will be measured against those expectations (KPIs and measures). At the end, they evaluate actual performance against those expectations using the KPIs and measures. In other words, a coach only coaches about 90% of the time.

PPAs are signed precisely by individuals because they are Performance Agreements. By signing it, a person commits. They are saying: "I will achieve this in this time frame".

A person's manager (designated leader) signs the PPA because they are also committing. They are saying, "This is what I expect you to deliver. Here is how I will measure your delivery at certain points in time. This will help you achieve when I am coaching you."

Signatures on PPA can be electronic or manual. (The work flow that implements this policy will clarify these requirements).

4. **The PPA Cascade**

PPA's are implemented using a CASCADE DOWN approach at SAMPLE CO. They translate SAMPLE CO.'s Next Year's Strategic Direction, Next Year's Tactical Operating Plan, Next Year's New Initiatives / Business Improvement Project Book and Next Year's Operating and Capital Financial Plan into specific performance objectives for individuals. This starts at the CEO / EVP level and cascades down the reporting lines in each EVP's area of responsibility.

Next Year's PPA cascade starts the day that the Board approves SAMPLE CO. Next Year's Plan and Budget, although much preparatory work can happen based on last year's cycle.

Note: "Next Year's Strategic Direction, Next Year's Tactical Operating Plan, Next Year's New Initiatives / Business Improvement Project Book, Next Year's Operating and Capital Financial Plan" are all terms that are defined in SAMPLE CO. Annual Planning Cycle. Although they sound somewhat clumsy at first, they help keep us straight on the difference between this year's version of these and next year's. In practice, we will say concrete things like the 2008 Strategic Direction and the 2009 Strategic Direction. This is the language we use to talk about these things on a day-to-day basis.

5. **SAMPLE CO. Leaders are Responsible for Getting PPAs in Place**

Each SAMPLE CO. Leader is responsible for ensuring that PPA's exist by the following dates for all their direct reports. **The following dates are tentative. Each year, they need confirmation by the SAMPLE CO. Executive.**

CEO and EVP's   December 15th of each calendar year

EVPs' direct reports   December 31st of each calendar year

Individuals reporting to   January 15th following
people who report to EVP's   the December 31st above

Local Operating Leaders   July 15th before the start of the operating year

Staff in Assigned Roles   on the same cycle as their Manager-Leader

Staff Working on
 A Project by Project Basis   Within a week of the designated project or
                                             program start, updated as often as needed
                                             during the life of the project.

6. PPA Process and Service Support

The Human Resources group is accountable for:

- Operating the manual procedures and automated tools used to prepare, to sign and to file PPA's, including starter templates for PPA's that are related to Role Accountability Profiles and Job Descriptions.
- Providing training to SAMPLE CO. Leaders on the PPA process.
- Ensuring that a copy of each PPA for each individual is kept in a secure fashion.
- Providing as required / as requested personal support to any individual who encounters difficulty during the PPA preparation process.

The Business Analysis group in Financial Management is accountable for defining KPI's and doing the ongoing analysis and reporting which reports progress on them. Elements of their work will be incorporated in PPAs at various levels at SAMPLE CO.

The Business Analysis group in Organizational Capability is accountable for operating SAMPLE CO.'s annual Strategic Planning, Tactical Planning, and New Initiatives / Business Improvement Project planning and approval process. Elements from the records developed during these processes will feed into individual PPA's for SAMPLE CO. Leaders.

The Financial Analysis group in Financial Services is accountable for operating the SAMPLE CO.'s annual Operating and Capital Budget process, as well as reporting on SAMPLE CO.'s financial performance on an ongoing basis. Elements from their work will feed into individuals PPA's and PPE's of SAMPLE CO. Leaders.

7. PPA Complexity

PPA's for senior leaders will be more complex, and contain more elements than PPAs for individuals closer to operating level. This simply reflects the greater scope and responsibility associated with their jobs.

PPAs at the operating level will be short - 1 or 2 pages. PPAs for individuals at the various management levels will be longer, containing more elements. This length and complexity will reflect the scope of the job.

8. Generic Elements for SAMPLE CO. Leaders

SAMPLE CO. Managers will have a number of standard accountabilities and measures added to their PPA's. See the table below for detail.

In each case, this generic language will be made concrete by reference to specific numbers or items in accounting records or project records or planning records.
Generic PPA Elements for SAMPLE CO. Leaders

This includes individuals who have staff reporting to them, and who manage budget/capital budgets and expenditures.

Initiating Conditions	Objective	KPI's or Measure	Notes
Individuals have people reporting to them	Manage the individual performance of direct reports	Next Year's PPA's exist for each person by the dates required This Year's Personal Performance Evaluations (PPE's) exist for each direct report by the date required	A competent manager will simply use a PPA and a PPE as bookends on an on-going process of performance feedback that occurs throughout the year.
Individual has fiscal authority over either capital or operating expenditures	Manage the financial performance of the area over which the individual has responsibility	The following exist by the dates required SAMPLE CO.'s annual planning cycle: - Next Year's Tactical Plan for the group, - Next Year's New Initiatives / Improvement Project Plans (if any) -Next Year's Operating and Capital Financial Plan for this group Expenditures are within Budget over the course of the year; Variances that relate to operating differences (as opposed to	Business Analysis in Organizational Capability is accountable for operating the Tactical Planning and the New Initiatives / Improvement Project development and approval process. Financial Analysis in Financial Services is accountable for operating the Financial Planning and Reporting process. They generate the specific measures in these areas by which these

Initiating Conditions	Objective	KPI's or Measure	Notes
		accounting timing and coding issues) are explained or corrected by year-end.	measures are made concrete.
Individual has responsibility for acting as business sponsor for the execution of an approved New Initiative / Business Improvement Project	Oversee the successful completion of the X New Initiative / Business Improvement Project	A project plan and budget that aligns with SAMPLE CO.'s Project Authority, Management, and Execution Policy exists. Target dates in the project plan are met. Project expenditures stay within the project budget. Progress reporting is carried out in a way that is aligned with SAMPLE CO.'s Project Authority, Management and Execution Policy	Financial Services and the Project Office in Organizational Capability will need to provide information that makes these measures concrete.

Appendix Two: Sample Personal Performance Evaluation Policy

PERSONAL PERFORMANCE EVALUATION POLICY

Purpose:

To govern the process by which SAMPLE CO. Leaders evaluate the personal performance of all SAMPLE CO. individuals.

Note:
Personal Performance Evaluation is abbreviated PPE.

Individual contractors who do work for SAMPLE CO. on a time defined based (start date and end date) also need some type of performance evaluation. However, this process is a separate and independent one. The purpose of these contractor performance evaluations is to provide information to other SAMPLE CO. leaders who may be considering these individuals. A separate policy and work flow for these individuals will be developed at a future date.

Principles:

1. **Performance Evaluation Cannot Occur without the existing of a relevant Personal Performance Agreement**

   Performance evaluation must be based on concrete measures and KPI's (key performance indicators – expressed in numbers) to be effective, not subjective perception. To ensure this, the completion of a Personal Performance Evaluation (PPE) therefore requires the prior completion of a Personal Performance Agreement (PPA) with the individual being evaluated.

2. **PPE's and Calendar Dates**

   A PPA is for a specific individual for a specific period. SAMPLE CO. has several "natural" calendar cycles. PPA time periods need to consider these.

   - The operating **or operating year runs** from September to August. A number of the significant operating points in it are tied to events in the operating year (semester start, major holidays – e.g. Thanksgiving, Christmas, Spring Break etc, and summer o). Individuals who work at the local service locations are most exposed to this cycle. Trends in operating and financial KPIs for this group of staff are often most meaningful on a month-by-month, current operating year to past operating year basis.

   - The fiscal year is aligned with the calendar year – January to December. SAMPLE CO. Leaders and staff in Head Office experience much of their work structured around calendar dates – month end, quarter end, year-end. Trends for this group of staff are often most meaningful on a month by month, current fiscal year to past fiscal year basis

- **Project or program** cycle – which have a start and target date, often referred to as sunrise and sunset days. KPIs and other performance measures are often most meaningful on a "comparison to targeted" milestone date basis.

Generally, PPAs that reflect the operating year are most appropriate for local operating staff.

PPAs that reflect the fiscal year are most appropriate for SAMPLE CO. managers and Head Office staff.

Project based PPAs are most appropriate for individuals who work primarily on projects (e.g. IT professionals and individuals assigned to projects).

PPE timing will therefore be matched with the calendar cycle used to prepare the PPA, which is the basis of the performance evaluation.

This has several business benefits:

- Not all PPEs have to be completed close to calendar year end (which is a busy period for other business reasons).

- Individuals who have PPAs related to a project lifetime will have a PPE completed with 2 weeks of project completion.

At the minimum, each SAMPLE CO. individual will receive at least one PPE in a calendar year.

3. PPE's are Reports of An Individual's Accomplishments as Evidenced by Measures and KPI's

Since PPA's contain concrete measures (happened or did not happened) and numerical KPI/s (numbers and ratios), evaluation is straightforward. Individuals either succeeded or not.

Questions of judgment enter the evaluation process in the comments that describe or expand on situations where an individual did not succeed on a measure or KPI. Those comments deal with "degree of achievement" and "extenuating circumstances", if they exist. The qualitative comments boxes on PPE forms exist to allow Managers to deal with these needs. **However, they cannot replace the fundamental report on the yes / no nature of basic accomplishment of the measure / KPI.**

Individuals can also exceed measures or KPI's. Again, the qualitative comment boxes exist to allow Managers to comment on quantitative or qualitative overachievement.

Because of the fundamental "achieved or not achieved" nature of the measures and KPI's, individuals can largely self evaluate their performance.

4. An SAMPLE CO. Leader's Responsibility to Effectively Take Both Coaching and Performance Evaluation Stances

Each SAMPLE CO. individual has a person who is that individual's designated coach. Normally, a person's manager is also that person's coach. The Manager has several responsibilities with respect to each employee in their area of responsibility.

- Establishing an appropriate PPA with each employee at the beginning of the performance period.

- Holding regular coaching sessions with each employee in which Managers:

   ○ review the employee's performance to-date by reviewing status reports on KPIs, Measures, and Evidence of Accomplishment with the employee.

   ○ coach the employee on ways in which they can improve their delivery and performance, particularly if KPIs and Measures trends indicate that the employee will not deliver agreed to results.

   ○ help the employee develop their personal skills and competencies in a broader way.

- Evaluating the person's delivery and contribution to SAMPLE CO. at the end of the PPA period.

During the last responsibility, the coach moves out of a coaching stance and takes on the stance of performance evaluator. As performance evaluators, Managers must place SAMPLE CO. first in their mind. They must review the person's delivery during the performance period from the perspective **of the value that it has contributed to SAMPLE CO.**

5. The Summary Performance Measure

An individual's execution and delivery will be rated once a year by the person to whom that the individual reports. The purpose of this rating is to summarize the individual's accomplishments in the past performance period against the agreed to KPIs, Measures and Evidence of Accomplishment associated with each performance objective in the PPA.

The NORMAL rating is "Performance Achieved Most or All Performance Measures". (See the details of the scale that follow.) Most individuals will be rated at this point on the scale. Only a few individuals will receive ratings at the top or bottom of the scale.

This rating reflects that the fact that PPA performance objectives are set at reasonable levels, and describe what an individual has to do this period to meet **SAMPLE CO.**'s expectations of their normal performance.

6. **The Rating Scale**

5 Performance Dramatically Exceeded Performance Measures

This employee has delivered at a level that has exceeded all Measures in the employee's PPA – perhaps even doubling the delivery expected on the majority or most of them.

4 Performance Exceeded Some Performance Measures

This employee has delivered at a level that has met all of the KPIs, Measures and Evidence of Accomplishments at the expected level, and has exceeded delivery on at least half of them, particularly on those of the most importance or weight.

3 Performance Achieved Most or All Performance Measures

This employee has delivered at a level that meets most or all of the KPIs and Measures.

If the employee has not achieved on one or two of the Measures, it is clear that events beyond the employee's control have kept him / her from doing so. The employee **has communicated** with you during your coaching sessions about this potential lack of delivery. The individual **has clearly taken actions** intended to correct the situation.

2 Execution Does Not Meet 50% of Performance Measures

This employee has delivered at a level that has not delivered on 50% of the Measures. There are no clear reasons for this other than the individual's own performance. This pattern has become clear over the course of the year during your coaching sessions. The employee initiated dialogue with you about these issues, and was proactive about taking steps to reverse this situation. There is clear evidence that things are on an improving trend. This pattern will not be repeated.

1   Execution Is Severely Below Performance Measures

This employee has delivered at a level that has not most or all of the Performance Measures. There are no clear reasons for this other than the individual's own performance. The individual **has not communicated** with others about this potential lack of delivery, and has not taken **actions** to correct the situation.

During your coaching sessions during the performance period, the employee has been available to change their performance to reverse this pattern. The employee might have attempted but shown little or no sign of success.
You cannot leave this employee this in position, but must take remedial action.

In most cases, the "Performance Achieved Most or All Performance Measures" rating will apply.

7.   SAMPLE CO. Leaders are Responsible for Doing PPE's

Each SAMPLE CO. Leader is responsible for that a PPE is completed within TWO WEEKS of the end of the PPA period for each employee in his or her area of responsibility.

For most individuals, this means that at least once PPE will be completed each year. However, it is possible that multiple PPE's could be done for an individual. In this case, there will be multiple PPA's, either linked to calendar periods that are shorter than a year, or to project start and start dates.

8.   PPE Process and Service Support

The Human Resources group in is accountable for:

- Providing the manual procedures and automated tools used to prepare, to sign, and to file PPE's.

- Ensuring that a copy of the each PPE for each individual is kept in a secure fashion.

- Providing as required / as requested personal support to any individual who encounters difficulty during the PPE completion process.

- Acting as "dispute resolvers" when the PPE completion process results in a difference in perceptions between an individual and the person to whom that person reports.
- Providing support to SAMPLE CO. Leaders on their actions to respond to individuals who are either the top or the bottom of the Summary Rating.

The Business Analysis group in Financial Management is accountable for providing information on SAMPLE CO. wide KPI's and doing the ongoing analysis and reporting which reports progress on them. Elements of their work will be incorporated in PPE's at various levels at SAMPLE CO.

The Financial Analysis group in Financial Management is accountable for operating the SAMPLE CO.'s annual Operating and Capital Budget process, as well as reporting on SAMPLE CO.'s financial performance on an ongoing basis. Elements from their work related to financial execution will be PPE's of SAMPLE CO. Leaders whose PPA's include financial performance Measures.

9. Employees Can Disagree with Manager's Summary Ratings of their Performance

SAMPLE CO.'s PPA / PPE processes require a designated Manager to hold regular coaching sessions with each employee in their area of responsibility. During these sessions, the employee and the Manager will review performance progress to-date by discussing the reported trends in KPIs, as well as the status of Measures and of Evidence of Accomplishments.

If this is done, there will be few surprises at PPE time. The existence of a KPI or a Measure or an Evidence of Accomplishment for each performance objective means that the employee will have the ability to self-evaluate their performance throughout the performance period. The regular discussion of progress on these during coaching sessions means that the employee will be well aware of their overall level of performance. Therefore, the Manager's Summary Performance Rating should be expected by the employee.

However, employees may disagree with their Manager's summary rating. In this case, the employee will sign the PPE in a different place (see format later on in this document). As well, the employee will be required to write a note indicating the reasons for the disagreement. This note should be attached to the final PPE.

10. SAMPLE CO. Leaders are Responsible for Following Up On 5 & 1 Level PPE Summary Ratings

SAMPLE CO. Leaders will take action to follow up in the ways described below on the following PPE Performance Ratings.

Performance Rating	Objective	Action	Notes
5 **Performance Dramatically**	Identify the person as a potential High Performer.	Contact Human Resources to conduct a follow	In any given year, less than 5% of the individuals at a

Performance Rating	Objective	Action	Notes
Exceeded Performance Measures	Assess if the person also has High Potential. **High Performer**: Person may be capable of delivering in this fashion over a period of years. **High Potential**: Person's performance indicates a capability to deliver at normal plus levels in roles with substantially more scope and responsibility.	up meeting on this person's performance, suitability for other roles and long-term (more than 1 year) potential to contribute to SAMPLE CO. Human Resources will take responsibility for including this person in accelerated personal development programs and succession planning	given level will be in this group.
1 **Execution Is Severely Below Performance Measures**	Develop a personal development program (training and coaching) which increases the person's skill levels so that this rating will not be repeated in future. Or Initiate a career management program by which the individual is moved into a role where he or she can deliver at a normal or better level.	Contact Human Resources to conduct a follow up meeting. After this meeting, Human Resources will monitor the personal development program agreed to by the individual and the SAMPLE CO. Manager to whom the person reports. Or Human Resources will facilitate a job transition plan that places this person	SAMPLE CO.'s service promise to its customers cannot be met by individuals who continually deliver at this level. Unless a personal development program or a role re-assignment has an excellent chance of success, continued employment with SAMPLE CO. is in question for such individuals. **Such situations must be proactively managed by the**

Performance Rating	Objective	Action	Notes
		in a role in which the individual can deliver at normal plus levels.	**SAMPLE CO. Manager involved, with the support Human Resources.**

Final Words

In all the years that I have been working, I have yet to find a person who feels good or excited or motivated or energized by the performance appraisal process. Employee surveys, ones that I have commissioned, and ones that I have heard about by talking with professional colleagues, confirm this almost universal lack of enthusiasm for the appraisal process.

Yet it persists. I don't believe that something continues unless it serves a purpose.

My own experience shows that performance contracting, when well done, also serves those purpose. But it also achieves so much more. I was constantly amazed by the folks who took on the challenges of the measures, used them to self assess their performance, and then set out to beat those goals.

Not all of the folks who have worked for me when I use a performance contracting more optimistic and pleased about it. They were the folks who had difficulty performing. They did not enjoy having to be precise about what they were to do. They did not like the shared responsibility for continuously evaluating personal delivery against mutually agreed upon measures. They also hated being "appraised". So I have come to believe that their response was not a function of the performance contracting process. Rather it reflected who they were, and their general reluctance to be held accountable. They either moved on by themselves, or I moved them on. Hopefully, they found work environments where performance and delivery did not matter.

" I will try it; you know I like it" is the experience for most of the folks who I introduce to performance contracting. I hope that this is your experience too.

Roelf Woldring

Made in the USA
Charleston, SC
08 April 2013